SIMPLY
TOMATO

100 Recipes for Enjoying Your
Favorite Ingredient All Year Long

SIMPLY
TOMATO

Martha
Holmberg

Photographs by ELLEN SILVERMAN

 ARTISAN | New York

Library of Congress Cataloging-in-Publication Data

Names: Holmberg, Martha, author.
Title: Simply tomato : 100 recipes for enjoying your favorite ingredient
all year long / Martha Holmberg ; photographs by Ellen Silverman.
Description: New York : Artisan, [2023] | Includes index.
Identifiers: LCCN 2022037519 | ISBN 9781648290374 (hardback)
Subjects: LCSH: Cooking (Tomatoes) | Tomatoes. | LCGFT: Cookbooks.
Classification: LCC TX803.T6 H65 2023 | DDC 641.6/5642—dc23/eng/20220816
LC record available at https://lccn.loc.gov/2022037519

Design by Toni Tajima

Artisan books are available at special discounts when purchased in bulk for
premiums and sales promotions as well as for fundraising or educational
use. Special editions or book excerpts also can be created to specification.
For details, please contact special.markets@hbgusa.com.

The publisher is not responsible for websites (or their content) that are
not owned by the publisher.

The Hachette Speakers Bureau provides a wide range of authors for
speaking events. To find out more, go to hachettespeakersbureau.com
or email HachetteSpeakers@hbgusa.com.

Published by Artisan,
an imprint of Workman Publishing Co., Inc.,
a subsidiary of Hachette Book Group, Inc.
1290 Avenue of the Americas
New York, NY 10104
artisanbooks.com

Artisan is a registered trademark of Workman Publishing Co., Inc.,
a subsidiary of Hachette Book Group, Inc.

Printed in China on responsibly sourced paper

First printing, May 2023

10 9 8 7 6 5 4 3 2 1

This book is dedicated to all the
tomato breeders, seed savers, farmers,
mad scientists, pollinators, ladybugs,
and other creatures who make tomato
gardening fascinating and fun.
And to John and Charlotte,
who make life the same way.

CONTENTS

Welcome

I'm assuming that because you're reading this, you feel about tomatoes the way I do: you're crazy about them. Whether you grow your own or simply look forward to the first Cherokee Purple at the farmers' market, you feel a little ripple of joy when you hold a ripe tomato in your hand.

But lots of fresh vegetables and fruits are delicious, so what is it about tomatoes that inspires such passion in so many people? My theory is that we are first attracted by the sensuous color and shape of a tomato but then get hooked by the flavor, which is a complex dance between sweet, tangy, and that elusive umami flavor (more on that in a minute). And then there's the haunting fragrance of the leaves (see page 61).

Every year, I grow as many tomatoes as I can find space for, although I am not a very knowledgeable gardener. I skim the research, experiment with a few new ideas, talk to my plants (that's critical), and hope for the best. Fortunately for me, my tomato plants have always been obliging and rewarded me with pounds and pounds of beautiful fruit, which I spend the summer consuming in every way I can think of—in salads, soups cold and hot, gratins, tarts, drinks, pastas, pastas, and more pastas.

But this cookbook is devoted to cooking with tomatoes in all their forms, with recipes for using both fresh and canned tomatoes, of course, but also for what I think of as "semi-preserved" tomatoes: roasted tomatoes, tomato confit, pickled tomatoes, jams, tomato paste, and tomato water and syrup. Every year, I spend hours turning my tomatoes into these components, stashing them in the freezer, fridge, or cupboard to use in other dishes later in the year.

The benefit to these semi-preserved forms isn't that they keep a long time, it's that they're so dang good and fun to make. The transformation of a tomato's fresh delicate raw character into something beyond— deeper, chewier, sweeter—is one more of the daily miracles that make home cooking so satisfying.

What's not in this book is the most basic of preserving methods—canning. You can find countless resources for that in books and online, and given that canning tomatoes for long storage on a shelf involves some food-safety risks and generally should be done using a pressure canner, I like to leave the instructions to the experts. One reliable source is the *Ball Blue Book Guide to*

Preserving; the 37th edition was published in 2015, and you can learn plenty from Ball's website (see Resources, page 239).

Doubling Down on Flavor

Researchers have identified hundreds of flavor compounds in tomatoes, about sixteen of which seem to create the unique "tomato" flavor. No one is quite sure which substances play what roles in creating flavor, and in any case, we as normal people can't see the compounds when we look at a tomato, so we won't be choosing between a Green Zebra and a Mr. Stripey based on their relative levels of 2-isobutylthiazole and geraniol. We make our choices by tasting.

The flavor element that I find most intriguing in a tomato is glutamate. This is the substance that contributes to umami flavor, which is best described as meaty or savory. Umami is now widely accepted as the "fifth flavor," flavor being the sensation that we perceive through the sensors on our tongues. You probably remember the diagram from elementary school: sweet, sour, salty, bitter—and now, umami. A perfect example of umami is the flavor of the meat juices on the bottom of a roasting pan. Other high-umami foods include aged cheeses, dried mushrooms, soy sauce, fish sauce, and nutritional yeast.

Unlike most fruits and vegetables, tomatoes are quite high in glutamate—typically 246 milligrams per 100 grams (mg/100 g) for a fresh raw tomato, around 600 mg/100 g for a dried tomato, and 750 mg/ 100 g for tomato paste—and the riper the tomato, the higher the level of glutamate. For comparison with other high-glutamate foods, dried mushrooms clock in at around 350 mg/ 100 g, aged Spanish jamón has around 500 mg/ 100 g, Vietnamese fish sauce has 1,300 mg/ 100g, and 4-year-old Parmigiano (yum) has a whopping 2,200 mg/100 g.

Glutamate isn't the only compound that adds umami. Meat and fish contain an umami-providing nucleotide called inosinic acid, which, when combined with glutamates, intensifies the savory flavor.

As I learn more about the interaction of glutamate-rich foods, I understand why dishes that create layers of umami from several of these ingredients are often my favorites. Tomato-Peach Salad with Lime-Ginger Dressing (page 88), which includes a dash of fish sauce, is a perfect example, as is Braised Beef Short Ribs with Tomato, Dried Porcini, and Red Wine (page 193), an umami triple threat of tomato paste, browned beef, and dried porcini.

How This Book Is Organized

Simply Tomato is divided into predictable—though slightly arbitrary—chapters, from snacks and drinks to pastries. (Sorry, no desserts.) I say "arbitrary" because I've got Susie's Tomato and Zucchini Gratin (page 206) in the side dish chapter, but I've enjoyed many a dinner eating that gratin as my main dish, and on a hot day, a bowl of ice-cold gazpacho—in the soups chapter—makes a fine main dish as well. Not to mention that a couple of G & T & Ts from the snacks and drinks chapter and a bag of potato chips constitute dinner in my house now and again. So if you don't find what you're looking for in one chapter, check the others or the index.

In each recipe, I list the form of tomato that I consider ideal, but when another form would also be delicious, I list that along with any modifications you might need to make to adapt the recipe.

My Thoughts on Recipes

I have been developing and writing recipes for more than thirty years, both for my own dishes and for talented chefs, where my role as a co-writer is to translate their inspiring restaurant creations into something a home cook would be happy to make. But even after all this time, my point of view on recipe writing is still evolving. While parts of a recipe look like a formula—precise measurements (including metric!), temperatures, technical terms—a useful recipe is anything *but* formulaic. The variables involved in cooking are endlessly shifting, from shopping for ingredients to choosing equipment to regulating your cooktop . . . not to mention that I love cilantro and you don't, and your idea of "mildly spicy" would have me reaching for the fire extinguisher.

And, of course, most of what we're cooking with is made by nature, with a wide range in how juicy, tender, stringy, bitter, spicy, and/or creamy your [fill in the blank] is.

So rather than write my recipes striving for the strictest precision, I write them with plenty of descriptions, hints, tips, and guidance so that you have the knowledge you need to accommodate the differences between your life and mine. I try to imagine the hundreds of choices and decisions a cook will make, from doing the mise en place to adding the final seasoning to a dish, and I call out those moments of inflection so that you can pay special attention to them.

Regardless of the ever-shifting variables in cooking, a few principles are constant. Please read the following guidelines so you can get the best possible outcome from the recipes in this book.

INITIAL READ-THROUGH: Please review the recipe before you start cooking. I know it's tempting to jump into a recipe sauté pans ablaze, especially when you're in a hurry, but ultimately you'll save time and angst by reading through the whole thing first. Start with the ingredients list, where much of the prep work takes place. This is called *mise en place*, meaning "put in place." You'll not only put ingredients and equipment in place, but you'll also wrangle them into the form the recipe requires, such as diced, drained, toasted, etc.

If a recipe entails a task that needs a big chunk of time, such as long cooling or overnight marinating, I signal that up front in the headnote so you don't get an unpleasant surprise. Nonetheless, reading through the entire process lets you understand how the whole flow will go.

SERVING SIZE: Honestly, what's a serving size? Who is doing the eating? What else are they going to eat for that meal, or on that day? I calculate servings by averaging what I think I (as a human on the smaller side) and my boyfriend (a larger-model human) would want to eat. But if I say a pasta dish serves two or three and you eat all of it yourself, bravo for you.

BURNER TEMPERATURE: I usually indicate whether your pan should be over low, medium, medium-high, or high heat, but these are relative terms. The heat coming from your burner when the dial is pointing to the middle—medium—may not be the same as mine.

And the burner is only half the equation, because all pans conduct heat differently, liquids evaporate at differing rates depending on the shape of the pan, and the list goes on. All that to say, don't obey my instructions to cook something on medium-high if it seems like your burner needs to be cranked up or down a notch in order to do what it's supposed to do—brown, sizzle, sear, or simmer.

COOKING TIME: One of the hardest things to quantify in cooking is how long to cook something. A familiar vignette in any cooking school is the student asking the chef "How long should I cook this?" and the chef responding "Until it's done." Annoying, yes,

but true. I find that the best way to determine doneness is by describing what I'm looking for. Browned just around the edges or all over? Simmered until syrupy? In every recipe, I try to give the clues that let you know it's time to do something—flip, take from the oven, add another ingredient—so while you should pay attention to the range of minutes I suggest (and set your timer), please use the cooking times as guidelines, not absolutes, and trust your senses.

TASTING (OR RATHER TASTE, ADJUST, TASTE AGAIN): I can't tell you how critical tasting is to your success with any recipe, and tasting begins before you even turn on the stove. I start by tasting my raw ingredients in order to get a baseline sense of their flavors before I begin to cook (okay, not all of them . . . not tasting the baking powder). If I've opened a new bottle of olive oil, I'll take a sip to see whether it's grassy, sharp, or nutty. When using fresh herbs, I'll nibble a leaf; sometimes basil can be kind of astringent, or maybe this bunch of cilantro has no flavor. I definitely always taste nuts, because they get rancid easily, and of course for the recipes in this book, I taste my tomatoes.

As for seasoning, it's impossible to prescribe exactly the right amount in a recipe, and more than impossible to know what you, the reader, prefer. Making the dish so that you like it, not me, is the goal . . . at least until you invite me over for dinner. My philosophy is that you should lightly season each component of a dish (the mirepoix, the braising liquid, the sauce, etc.) as it's being created, and then dial in the seasoning for the entire dish when you are getting ready to serve it.

Proper seasoning is sometimes overlooked in our haste to get things to the table (especially if kids or guests are milling about or the cook has been enjoying a glass of wine during cooking), but pausing and consciously tasting and adjusting seasonings is as much a part of cooking as is putting the chicken schnitzel in the skillet or adding the dressing to the salad. As you taste, think of what might make the balance of flavors better. I always want a tension between the leading flavors, some variation of salty, sweet, tangy, spicy, and umami (more about umami on page 10). And you should know that I like my food quite salty (please read about the differences in salt brands on page 16), I like a lot of acid in my food, and I can't tolerate chile heat, so those are the default settings in my recipes. You should feel free to recalibrate to your own tastes.

STORAGE TIME: If you aren't familiar with a recipe, it's helpful to know whether you should be reheating those leftovers the next day for lunch or whether you can wait a week and still enjoy the dish. In my recipes, I give an indication of how long a dish will keep well, but of course most fresh food doesn't last long; use your common sense.

Where storage times get murky is with freezing times. Once food is frozen, it's not going to spoil in the way food left too long in the fridge will, so you don't need to worry about food safety. However, frozen food isn't totally inert, and the eating qualities will suffer after too much time in the freezer. I find that most dishes I freeze are excellent when thawed and eaten within 2 to 3 months, and I try to remember what's in my freezer so I can work my way through it. That being said, I just ate a lamb tagine that had been in the freezer for a year, and it was mighty fine.

The key is freezing your food properly, ideally at or below 0°F (–18°C). Food freezes faster in colder temperatures, and the faster it freezes, the smaller the ice crystals inside it will be. Large ice crystals can rupture the cell walls, making foods lose their juices or get soggy as they thaw. I have a very basic inexpensive freezer in my garage that works brilliantly. It's not frost-free, which is a pain because once a year (um, maybe once every five years?), I need to defrost it. But when a freezer is self-defrosting, the temperature fluctuates, which is not good for your frozen casserole.

And of course, you must wrap your food well so it's protected from freezer burn, which happens when moisture that's frozen in the food transforms into vapor, in a process called sublimation, a weird form of drying out. Freezer-burned food isn't harmful, but the flavor and texture won't be optimal. And we're all about optimal flavor and texture.

A GOOD REASON TO BE LAZY AND NOT SEED YOUR TOMATOES

So many recipes call for peeling and seeding tomatoes, mainly to eliminate the textural annoyance of curling bits of skin or seeds between your teeth. I rarely bother with either peeling or seeding because I'm lazy, er, focused on essentials, but here's another reason to skip that step: the seeds and other interior parts of a tomato contain more of the key flavor compounds.

British chef and innovator Heston Blumenthal wondered about precisely this question—to seed or not to seed—and partnered with some researchers at the University of Reading in the United Kingdom. Their studies, which involved measuring glutamic acid levels as well as conducting a tomato taste test, found that the inner parts of a tomato (the seeds and surrounding gel) contained about three times the glutamic acid of the outer flesh, and the tasting panel confirmed that the inner samples were tastier as well. At last, scientific validation for lazy cooks like me.

Advice on Key Ingredients That Aren't Tomatoes

While the tomatoes are the stars of the show here, every ingredient you use contributes to the success of your dish, so I'm sharing some thoughts on a few key players that will make a big difference.

ALEPPO PEPPER: You'll see this seasoning in many of my ingredient lists, and if you're not yet familiar with this chile flake, I hope you'll have the chance to make its acquaintance. Aleppo pepper comes originally from the region around the city of Aleppo in Syria, but the devastation of war has disrupted the supply. Now much of the crop is grown in Turkey, and some production has even begun in the United States. A few years ago, my boyfriend tracked down Aleppo pepper seeds (which are also called Halaby), and we have been growing our own plants, drying the peppers, and crushing them into a seasoning ever since.

The appeal of Aleppo pepper to me is its mild heat level coupled with a fruity, yes, even tomatoey, flavor, reminiscent of sun-dried tomatoes . . . but with a kick. If you can't find Aleppo pepper, you can use regular chile flakes or cayenne pepper (both of which are much hotter than Aleppo pepper), or perhaps another interesting ground chile such as piment d'Espelette from the Basque region of France.

BUTTER: To the question "Should I use salted or unsalted butter?" my answer is "Yes." Meaning I just don't think it really matters which type you use unless the recipe calls for a *large* amount of butter, like more than 8 tablespoons (115 g)—or, of course, you are restricting your salt intake for a medical reason. As illustrated, the difference in the amount of salt found in 8 tablespoons unsalted butter and the equivalent amount of salted butter is not much more than 1 gram. A teaspoon of table salt weighs about 6 grams, so you can see that 1 gram either way won't change the overall balance of your dish, especially one that will ultimately be "salted to taste."

FLOUR: The recipes in this book were developed and tested using unbleached all-purpose flour. If you'd like to use whole wheat flour, you can safely swap about one-third the amount of all-purpose with whole wheat and get decent results, but to use more whole wheat, or other whole-grain flour, you should either do your own experimenting or find a whole wheat recipe that's similar to mine from another trusted source and make the rest of my recipe using that.

No matter what flour you use, proper measurement is key, and that's not as easy as it sounds. If you're using a dry measuring cup, which measures volume, the way you load the flour into the cup makes a difference. (Be sure not to use a liquid measuring cup, which has extra room at the top plus a pour spout, making it impossible to level off the flour.) If you drag your cup through the bag of flour to scoop it up and then level it off with the back of a knife (the scoop-and-sweep method), you'll probably get more flour in your cup than if you spooned the flour into the cup and then leveled it off (the spoon-and-sweep method). This second method is how I, and most other recipe writers, measure flour using volume.

But even when you use the spoon-and-sweep method, you can have variations from cup to cup. The best way to get accurate measurements every time is to use a scale. The recipes in this book list flour and many other nonliquid ingredients by volume in cups, and then also (in parentheses) by their weight in grams.

FRESH HERBS: I know that it's not always easy to find every type of fresh herb, and even if your grocery store carries what you're looking for, you might balk at paying $2.79 for a tired sprig of tarragon that's been entombed in a plastic package. So if I call for an herb that you don't have, it's usually safe to substitute another. Flat-leaf parsley, which is widely available, can play the role of just about any other herb. Just pay attention to whether the recipe asks for a tender herb or a tougher, hardy one (often quite resinous), because 1 cup of rosemary leaves will not give you the same result as 1 cup of cilantro leaves.

Here's how I categorize tender versus hardy:

TENDER	HARDY
Basil	Marjoram
Chervil	Oregano
Chives	Peppermint
Cilantro	Rosemary
Dill	Sage
Mint (unless it's peppermint)	Savory
	Thyme
Flat-leaf parsley	
Tarragon	

To store fresh herbs, first remove any twist ties, rubber bands, or other tags; pull off any leaves or stems that are wilted or are en route to wilted; and then wrap the bunch in a very lightly dampened paper towel. If the herbs are still wet from produce-aisle spritzing, use a dry paper towel. Pack the wrapped herbs in a zip-top bag or an airtight container. Check every few days and do triage, keeping only pristine leaves.

OLIVE OIL (AS IN EXTRA-VIRGIN OLIVE OIL): This is the fat I use most often, whether actually cooking with heat or simply dressing a dish. For cooking, use a moderately priced extra-virgin oil, of which you'll find many brands on the grocery shelves, though not all are actually extra-virgin, or very tasty. Olive oil isn't well regulated in the United States, so producers can get away with misleading labeling, but here are two that I use, which are reliably produced following methods similar to those set by European olive oil standards:

- California Olive Ranch (note that much of their oil now comes from other parts of the world, not California, but it's all pretty good)

- Séka Hills, produced by the Yocha Dehe Wintun Nation, the original inhabitants of the Capay Valley in Northern California

I also like having a "finishing oil" on hand, usually an Italian extra-virgin oil with a more assertive personality than my daily oil. I use this oil as the final drizzle on a platter of tomatoes, bowl of gazpacho, or pissaladière hot from the oven.

Remember that olive oil is an agricultural product, just like a tomato, and so freshness is key. Look for the harvest date on the bottle. The freshest oil will be dated from the most recent winter, as olives are usually harvested between November and January. Oils will be fine for more than one year, but their fragrance and other flavor nuances fade over time. And olive oil, like any oil, even something like canola oil that we think of as "shelf-stable," will become rancid, especially once it's open and exposed to light, air, and heat. Yes, I (like you, I'm guessing) keep my olive oil next to my stovetop, but that's the worst place to keep it! So taste your oil periodically, and if it doesn't taste fresh and fruity, ditch it and get a new bottle.

PARMIGIANO-REGGIANO: While there are multitudes of "parmesan cheeses" on the market, it is worth seeking out and paying for the real deal. Authentic Parmigiano-Reggiano from Italy has a deeply nutty, sweet, umami-laden flavor that the others don't come close to, and adding a little Parmigiano to a dish to boost its savoriness is a tactic I employ frequently. While the finest Parmigianos can clock in at $30 per pound and higher, Costco carries a true Parmigiano-Reggiano that's closer to $12 per pound and is reliably good.

Store your Parm properly to avoid it drying out and becoming too piquant. Wrap it in parchment and then put it in an airtight container. The layer of parchment keeps the cheese in much better condition than if it were wrapped in plastic alone.

SALT AND PEPPER: I've noted elsewhere in this book that I like my food on the salty side. I know that some people have to watch their salt consumption, but in general, being generous with salt in your cooking results in only good things, making flavors pop, balancing acid and sweetness, and, overall, helping ingredients become their best selves.

I used Diamond Crystal kosher salt (the stuff in the red box, widely available) when I developed these recipes, so if you are going to use a different salt, please note that you'll need to make some conversions!

Diamond Crystal is sort of "fluffy" (you can easily crush it between your fingers when you want to make it finer), so it takes up more room in your measuring spoon than other brands of kosher salt, and definitely more than table or fine salt.

One tablespoon of Diamond Crystal, which weighs about 8 grams, has only about half the "salting power" of most other granulations of salt, which can weigh up to 18 grams per tablespoon. So when I call for "1 teaspoon kosher salt," and you are using a fine salt or another brand of kosher salt, such as Morton, you should start with ½ teaspoon and adjust up from there.

DIAMOND CRYSTAL KOSHER SALT	MORTON'S or ANOTHER KOSHER SALT BRAND, or A FINE SALT
Weight per tablespoon:	
8 grams	18 grams
When a recipe calls for "1 teaspoon kosher salt" use:	
1 teaspoon	½ teaspoon and adjust from there

As for salt's frequent partner—"freshly ground black pepper"—please use a pepper mill and grind your own rather than use the preground spice, which loses its fragrance and bite so easily. Freshly ground black pepper, especially a good variety such as Tellicherry, brings a wonderful perfume to your dish that already ground pepper can't deliver.

Here's a tip: it's nearly impossible to grind black pepper directly into a measuring spoon, and grinding it onto a surface and then scooting it into the spoon is a pain. Using the pepper grinder you regularly reach for, figure out how many twists you need to grind a measured amount, say ¼ teaspoon, and then any time you need black pepper, you can simply count your twists.

With So Many Tomatoes, How to Choose the Right One?

If you've ever looked at the tomato pages in a seed catalog, you know the waters are deep when it comes to tomato varieties. Crimson, green striped, deep purple, chocolate brown, tiny and round, huge with pleated shoulders, slender torpedo shapes. And the names! Berkeley Tie Dye, Bloody Butcher, German Lunchbox, Hillbilly, Marvel Stripe, Mortgage Lifter, Mr. Stripey, Pink Ping Pong, Ten Fingers of Naples.

Every trip to the farmers' market is the chance to discover new tomatoes, and even a moderately ambitious mainstream grocery store will have close to a dozen types, between the various cherry tomatoes, the "tomatoes on the vine," and whatever the latest tomato in a plastic clamshell is. Overwhelming, in a good way.

We know we can't choose a good tomato by analyzing its flavor compounds without a detour to the science lab, so what strategies can we use to get the tomato that will be best for the dish we want to cook? Attributes such as size, shape, and juiciness all matter when choosing a tomato for a dish, but above all, I'd rank flavor.

The Part of Flavor That You <u>Can</u> See

A tomato's flavor will be affected by soil, nutrients, and climate—hello, terroir—and of course the distinct personality of each of the literally thousands of tomato varieties, so predicting the flavor of any particular tomato isn't easy. But we can generalize about flavor using color as an indicator of the levels of sugars and acids, as well as a few hard-to-quantify qualities. Experts don't all agree on this subject, but I'm a massive fan of Cynthia Sandberg, owner and farmer of Love Apple Farms in Santa Cruz, California, and these are her qualifiers.

RED TOMATOES tend to be fairly high in sugar and also high in acid, making them balanced but with a tart edge, which some people describe as "old-fashioned" flavor.

PINK TOMATOES are high in sugars, so they're perceived as sweet.

ORANGE AND YELLOW TOMATOES are low in acid, so their sweetness comes to the fore, but if they don't contain adequate sugar, they'll just be perceived as bland— which has been my experience with yellow and orange varieties except for Sungold cherry tomatoes, the sweetest little flavor bombs you could imagine. I'm not sure whether their color is influencing my perception, but I think Sungolds, which are a rich orange, have tangerine notes as part of their supersweet and fruity character.

BLACK AND PURPLE TOMATOES are balanced, with a taste that Sandberg calls "smoky barbecue flavor." I agree. I frequently grow two types of "black" tomato—Black Krims and Paul Robesons—and they definitely have a savory quality to them that is delectable.

GREEN (AS IN "GREEN WHEN RIPE") TOMATOES are sweet, as well as so pretty, and can have tropical notes, including those of guava and pineapple.

General Tomato Terminology

Beyond color, tomatoes can be sorted into some broad buckets, and it's useful to understand the terms used for those categories, which you may come across at the farmers' market, in recipes, or at the grocery store.

The first bucket is the manner in which the tomato was propagated: hybrid or heirloom.

HYBRID: These tomatoes are varieties that were bred by intentionally cross-pollinating different varieties in order to get specific attributes, such as disease resistance or greater crop yield—good things, right? But hybrid tomatoes are also bred for characteristics that help them withstand shipping and have a long shelf life—not so good, because those attributes are usually at odds with good flavor or texture.

But hybrid doesn't always mean inferior. Many favorites for home gardeners and market farmers are hybrids, such as Early Girls and Sweet 100s, which are both delicious and reliable tomatoes that are always welcome in my garden. Something to note: if you save seeds from hybrid tomatoes and plant them, you won't get that same type of tomato; you need to start with commercially bred seeds every year.

HEIRLOOM: The term refers to a tomato variety that has not been crossbred with other varieties, and though there's not one governing body that grants heirloom status, the generally accepted qualification is a tomato variety whose seeds have been passed down for at least fifty years by a family or a religious, ethnic, or tribal group, and I'm assuming this can include the many seed-saving organizations out there, such as Seed Savers Exchange. Tomato types that were crossbred commercially before 1940 are also often considered heirloom. Heirlooms are open-pollinated, which means pollination happens naturally, and if the seeds are saved and planted next year, they will produce the same type of tomato.

For many growers and cooks, heirloom tomatoes are where the action is, due to the vast variety in color, shape, size, and flavor.

The most important thing for a cook to know, however, is that just as hybrid doesn't always equal bad, heirloom doesn't always equal good. Over the last decade, I've seen an increase in the number of "heirloom tomatoes" at grocery stores. They look promising—voluptuously misshapen, multicolored—but most end up having no flavor and an icky, pulpy texture. They're not much better than regular crappy grocery store tomatoes, but they cost $2 more per pound. Unless you've had the chance to taste a sample, steer clear of generic heirloom.

Other tomato terminology refers to the shape and size of the tomato. Here are some common descriptors.

BEEFSTEAK: An iconic tomato type, beefsteaks are large—frequently weighing 2 pounds (900 g) or more, though typically closer to 12 ounces (340 g). The name, according to noted seed breeder Craig LeHoullier, originated in an 1869 seed catalog that touted the tomato as being as "solid and meaty as a beefsteak." Slightly flattened, often with gently ribbed shoulders, beefsteaks have small seed pockets, which means dense flesh that is good for slicing. The name "beefsteak" can refer to an actual variety or to a class of tomato that includes heirlooms such as the popular Brandywine, as well as my favorite, Black Krim.

CHERRY: The little guys. There are many varieties and brands at the grocery store, as well as of course in seed catalogs, and grocery store cherry tomatoes are usually the only mass-market tomatoes with any spark of life to them. While rarely brilliant, they almost always at least have some acid and a flavor that reminds you of a homegrown summer tomato. This is due to the fact that even when ripe, cherry tomatoes are sturdy and can be packed and shipped without damage, so they are allowed to ripen on the plant before picking.

COCKTAIL: This is a commercial designation that means bigger than a cherry, smaller than a full-size tomato. I think cocktail is a nice size for tomatoes that will be part of a tossed green salad; a quarter of a cocktail tomato is perfectly bite-size.

GRAPE: These oblong little tomatoes are thick skinned, with dense, not very juicy flesh but a sweet flavor. Sales of grape tomatoes have outpaced those of traditional cherry tomatoes over the last couple of decades, and if you have any little kids in the house, you understand why, as grape tomatoes are super snackable and don't squirt juice when you bite into them.

ON THE VINE: This is the term for tomatoes that are sold commercially with their stems attached, purportedly because intact stems preserve the fragrance of the tomato (which aligns with what I've learned about volatile aroma compounds with regard to refrigeration; see page 84), but I think the "vines" are mostly for aesthetic appeal. You'll find both large tomatoes and cherry tomatoes on the vine. Magazine food stylists love them!

OXHEART: Similar to beefsteaks, oxhearts are very large and meaty, with a distinctive pointed end, so the tomato resembles a heart. Why the heart of an ox in particular, I'm not sure! Oxhearts are usually red or pink, though other colors have been developed. My favorite variety is called Cuore di Bue (beef heart, in Italian), which I've grown for a few years and find delightful, both because of its shape and size (most of mine have weighed close to 1 pound/450 g), but also because the dense, sweet flesh is excellent for sauces.

PLUM, ROMA, OR PASTE: These are the smallish oval tomatoes with dense flesh and not much in the way of seeds, grown and used primarily for making sauces and tomato paste. Plum tomatoes from the grocery store are every bit as dull and dry as their round compatriots, almost all of which are picked green for transport, then treated with ethylene gas to force "ripening," which mostly means softening and turning red but not developing much in terms of flavor. But even pedestrian grocery store plum tomatoes respond well to roasting (see page 164).

The most famous plum tomato is the San Marzano, grown in Italy near Mount Vesuvius and protected by special government status. I've grown San Marzano tomatoes from seed in my garden (which is not near Mount Vesuvius) and they were indeed delicious, though most of them were afflicted with blossom-end rot, a calcium imbalance caused by watering problems . . . the watering problems caused by me. To me, San Marzanos are the heartbreak tomato, except when they are canned. Learn about canned San Marzanos on page 27.

PEAR: You'll most often see yellow cherry-size pear tomatoes, though red pears and other colors exist. Some pear tomatoes are heirlooms and others are popular commercial hybrids.

SLICER: No mystery here; a slicer is simply a tomato that's good for slicing and putting on something delicious like a BLT. Large beefsteaks are sometimes called slicers, but to me, the large slices of a beefsteak end up being unwieldy. I like Early Girls or other tomatoes that produce a slice with a 2- to 3-inch (5 to 7.5 cm) diameter.

It's Okay to Buy Tomatoes at the Grocery Store

I have the luxury of plentiful garden space and a flexible schedule, two essentials for ensuring a supply of ripe tomatoes fresh from your own vines. I've also lived in cities with farmers' markets every day of the week as well as grocery stores that buy from local producers, so for most of my cooking life over the last two decades, in the summer, I've been eating "real" tomatoes.

But I know this isn't true for everyone. Whether it's the lack of a backyard or big patio, demands on your time that don't allow spending hours in a garden, or just living in an area with nothing more than generic grocery stores, many forces can conspire against a tomato-loving cook, preventing you from having easy access to baskets of Paul Robesons, Mortgage Lifters, or Tigerellas. And then, of course, there's winter, when even residents of the Garden of Eden can't get a ripe tomato.

Fortunately, some grocery store tomatoes are better than others. Among the dreary pale red orbs with cottony white interiors are some varieties that are quite good, with a balance of sugars and acids, and juicy but firm textures. These are generally "branded" tomatoes that come from big companies that spend years and zillions of dollars developing and marketing them to us consumers.

Here are three of the most widely distributed "name-brand" tomatoes to look for. I buy all of these when local tomatoes aren't in season, and I've tested many of the recipes in this book with them as well.

CAMPARI: These were developed back in the 1990s by a Dutch seed company, Enza Zaden, though I've seen them only in the Northwest of the United States, where I live, for the last five years or so. According to the Canadian company that currently markets them, Camparis are grown hydroponically in greenhouses, without pesticides, and they are allowed to fully ripen before picking and aren't blasted with ethylene gas to force ripening, like so many commercial tomatoes.

Camparis are between a cherry and a slicer, about the size of a golf ball. They're tomato-red and round, and often come with the stems still attached. The downside of Camparis is their plastic clamshell packaging, of which the world has way too much. But the upside is that they taste darned good! Well balanced between sweet and acid, they also have that elusive "tomato" flavor and a firm texture; they are easy to slice but juicy and never pulpy. I recommend Camparis especially for salads and roasting.

JACOBS FARM DEL CABO: Organically grown on the Baja peninsula and in neighboring Mexican states, these tomatoes are field grown, not raised in greenhouses, which, according to the company, puts the kind of stress on the growing plant that results in more complex flavor. The company started with cherry tomatoes, and now I see many varieties, from yellow pear to cocktail on the vine, and more. I find that Del Cabo tomatoes have generally very good flavor, though I've had a few meh ones, and I often find a few spoiled tomatoes hiding out in the packages, so always check before you buy.

KUMATO: These chocolate-brown tomatoes were developed by plant breeder Luis Ortega Fernández for Swiss agribusiness giant Syngenta in the early 2000s. Kumatos are medium in size, round, and a beautiful rich brown-to-burgundy-to-green. Like a Campari, they have a great sugar-to-acid balance, the flesh is firm and silky, and they slice beautifully.

AN OPERATOR'S MANUAL FOR FRESH TOMATOES

Here's a quick reference on storing and prepping your gorgeous fresh tomatoes.

RIPENING

If a tomato has begun to ripen on the vine, it will continue to ripen indoors. Early ripening is indicated by a flush of pink and a texture that gives a tiny bit when squeezed. Keep your ripening tomato in a warm but not hot spot with plenty of air circulation. A windowsill is fine as long as the sun exposure isn't intense.

STORING

Store fresh tomatoes at cool room temperature in a breathable container, such as a paper bag or a box. Avoid plastic bags, which can hasten their demise through captured humidity and ethylene gas produced by the tomatoes themselves. If you've piled your tomatoes into a bowl, which of course looks fabulous, be sure to monitor them in case one is beginning to rot, which can quickly spoil them all.

If your environment seems too warm, you have fruit flies, or there are other factors that prevent storage on the counter, it's fine to refrigerate your tomatoes, despite what you may have heard about cold temperatures muting their flavors. The flavor compounds will be affected only by cold temperatures after about 3 days (see page 84).

SLICING

Although tomatoes are delicate and juicy, their skins will resist all but the sharpest of knives, so to get the cleanest cuts—and enjoy the sensual process of slicing through a ripe tomato—you need to use a very sharp knife with a thin blade. Some knives designed for tomatoes are serrated, which helps grab the skin and split it open as you begin to slice (a fine-bladed bread knife will also work well), but whether serrated or plain, sharpness is key. I reserve one of my knives for tomatoes only.

CORING

In almost all cases, you want to cut out the core (the spot where the tomato was attached to the vine), which is edible but slightly tough and not tasty. To core a tomato, insert the tip of a sharp paring knife close to the core at a slight angle and cut in a circle around the core, popping it out with the knife. Underripe tomatoes will be whitish around the core, so use this as an opportunity to cut away any underripe flesh.

SEEDING

Tomato seeds are organized in small pockets spaced throughout the denser tomato flesh. The juicy gel that surrounds the seeds is highly flavorful, but sometimes you don't want the texture of the seeds in your dish and so you need to remove them.

An easy way to seed a tomato is to cut it in half horizontally (along what would be the equator if the tomato were Earth), revealing most of the seed pockets. Gently squeeze each half until the seeds come out, taking care not to deform the tomato halves too much.

A more thorough method involves peeling the tomatoes first; see below.

PEELING

When eating a fresh tomato, you rarely notice the skin, other than to admire its pretty color. But when tomatoes are cooked, the skins can become annoying little scrolls, a chewy textural distraction. I don't always peel my tomatoes, but if I'm making a dish that demands some refinement, I take the extra step.

To peel a fresh tomato, bring a large pot of water to a boil and set up a bowl of ice water. Core the tomato and cut an X in the blossom end; this will allow the skin to curl away from the body. Drop the tomato into the boiling water and then, after a few seconds, retrieve it with tongs or a slotted spoon. If the skin has loosened, transfer the tomato to the ice water. If not, let it boil another few seconds. The goal is to cook only a thin layer of flesh just below the skin, which allows the skin to release but doesn't partially cook the tomato. A very ripe tomato may need only 5 to 10 seconds of boiling, while a firmer one needs 30 seconds or more.

When the tomato is cool enough to handle, use your fingers or the paring knife to peel away the skin.

To seed the peeled tomato, insert your finger or the tip of the paring knife into the tomato, locate a seed pocket, and scoop out the seeds. Repeat until you've emptied all the pockets.

DICING

Dicing a tomato can be tricky because
(1) you're trying to cut square shapes from a round fruit and (2) the interior isn't uniform, due to the pockets of juice and seeds.

If perfect squares aren't important, simply cut your tomato into small chunks: cut it into wedges from stem end to blossom end and then cut the wedges into pieces.

For a more perfect shape—for example, if you're using diced tomato as a garnish—use only the fleshy "cheeks." With a sharp knife, cut from stem end to blossom end following the curve of the fruit and slicing off only the flesh, leaving the seed pockets and ribs behind.

Work your way around the tomato, ending up with four or five pieces of seedless flesh, along with what's left of the interior, which you could use for making tomato water, a broth, or anything else where you don't mind seeds.

Cut the tomato cheeks into strips and then cut across the strips into dice.

Canned Tomatoes Aren't Second-Class Citizens

Growing up, I ate many a canned green bean, cling peach (in heavy syrup!), and mushy serving of canned "petits pois." Those fruits and vegetables are indeed poor imitations of their fresh originals, but a canned tomato is a different story—it has integrity and its own identity. While you can't really make a salad using a canned tomato, you can achieve all manner of other deliciousness.

The challenge with a canned tomato, however, is that unlike a fresh one that you can see, smell, even squeeze (gently, surreptitiously), a canned tomato is hidden inside a can . . . hopefully a recyclable steel, BPA-free one.

So how do you know which ones to buy? Not only are canned tomatoes produced by many brands, but they also come in many forms—whole peeled, with or without basil, garlic, and/or chiles. Diced. Petite diced. Crushed. Pureed. Stewed. Even fire-roasted, for gosh sake.

I define these various forms of tomato on the following pages, but I'll cut to the chase and say that I (mostly) use only whole peeled tomatoes. Whether the intended result of your recipe is a smooth tomato puree or tomatoes cut into small bits, it's best to start with whole peeled tomatoes, with no other flavorings except salt, and do the shape-shifting yourself rather than buy the tomatoes already in a more manipulated form.

First of all, I don't have room in my kitchen cabinets to stock more than one type of canned tomato. But I also feel that I have more control when starting with the least processed form of canned tomatoes, and I can avoid surprises due to variation among brands, such as finding that my "crushed" tomatoes are as liquidy as tomato puree, or the "diced" tomatoes I added to my chili never soften properly or are not the size of dice that I wanted for my dish.

Coaxing canned whole tomatoes into the shape and size you want can be a bit sloppy, but you can mitigate the mess with the following strategies:

WHEN ALL YOU NEED IS SLIGHTLY SMALLER PIECES: Break the whole tomatoes up while they're still in the can. Either take a sharp knife and slice through them several times, or use your kitchen scissors to snip them into pieces. Be sure the hinge of your scissors is clean, because you'll be submerging them in the tomato juices. (Yes, I see what's in your junk drawer.)

WHEN YOU WANT UNIFORM CHUNKS OR FINELY CHOPPED TOMATOES: Take the whole tomatoes out of the can and gently "squeegee" each tomato with your fingers to remove excess liquid. Then lay them on your cutting board and customize the size and shape.

WHEN YOU WANT THE TOMATOES TRULY BROKEN UP: To take the whole tomatoes even further so they can be integrated into a braise or soup, pour them into a big bowl and squish them with your hands. Messy, but effective . . . and therapeutic!

And regardless of how you are chopping, snipping, or squishing, pay attention to the stem end and core of the tomato. Most tomatoes are very soft and will easily break apart during cooking, but sometimes you get a batch with a tough, stringy core; the stem end of almost every tomato is dense, so chop or crush the tough sections before you add the tomatoes to your dish.

Transfer any leftover canned tomatoes directly to the freezer. They freeze well, so if you don't need the entire can, slide the excess into a freezer container, label with the measured amount and the date, and freeze for later use.

THE SAN MARZANO MYSTIQUE

It might seem funny to think of a canned tomato as being famous, but indeed one type has achieved a sort of cult status: the San Marzano. Grown in the volcanic soil around Mount Vesuvius, between Naples and Salerno in the Campania region of Italy, the San Marzano (the name of both the tomato variety and the canned product) is a slender plum-type tomato with thick flesh, few seeds, low acidity, and rich flavor.

Like many European foods, authentic canned San Marzano tomatoes have DOP status, meaning they are allowed to display a mark certifying that they are the correct tomato type, grown in a designated area under strict guidelines for cultivating, harvesting, and packing. DOP stands for Denominazione d'Origine Protetta, and the system is a way of controlling the quality of the product, along with its ability to command a high price. A genuine can of San Marzano tomatoes will be labeled "Pomodoro San Marzano dell'Agro Sarnese Nocerino DOP" and will include a certification number as well.

But any time an ingredient fetches a premium price, beware. You may see "San Marzano" or "San Marzano-style" on a label, meaning the variety is San Marzano but it could have been grown anywhere. It may be delicious, but it's not a true San Marzano. The organization that governs San Marzano production claims that only around 5 percent of the San Marzanos sold in the United States are genuine, a claim that is entirely possible given that there are no regulations in the States that prevent a seller from sticking a DOP label on a can. Note that true San Marzanos will only be whole peeled or halved tomatoes—no diced, crushed, or other forms.

Are San Marzanos truly superior? You'll need to do your own taste test to decide. As with any agricultural product, some variation in quality is normal.

A Brief Lexicon of Canned Tomatoes

You won't find as many varieties of canned tomato as you will fresh; nonetheless, it's easy to get overwhelmed by the various forms of tomatoes-in-cans in the grocery store. Here's a guide to the most common products.

WHOLE PEELED: The least processed and the most versatile, these are ripe tomatoes that have been peeled and packed either with their own juices or with a tomato puree. The peeling is done by running the tomatoes through a lye bath, which is cheap and efficient, or by steam-peeling them, which feels much nicer to me. Check the label. All organic peeled tomatoes *must* be steam-peeled.

My preference is the lighter "with juice" style, which has a fresher, less-cooked flavor than those packed with puree. Most brands add a bit of salt, and perhaps a basil leaf, which I don't think interferes with the tomato flavor. But beware of brands that include calcium chloride, a substance used to keep the tomatoes firm—which is actually a problem, because keeping the tomatoes firm, it discourages them from breaking down and integrating into your dish.

DICED: Usually packed with calcium chloride so they keep their shape, diced tomatoes are more "chunked" than "diced," so don't expect a clean, uniform cut, and don't expect a diced tomato to soften up the way a fresh or whole canned tomato would. The one widely available brand that does not add the firming agent to its chopped tomatoes is Pomì, though the texture of their "chopped" is what you'll get if you chop your own whole canned tomatoes—slightly sloppy irregular chunks. Like real food.

PETITE DICED: Diced. But petite.

STEWED: These are tomatoes cooked with other flavorings, such as onions, chiles, and herbs. My mom probably cooked with stewed tomatoes, but I don't see any need for them; I'll add my own flavorings, thank you.

CRUSHED: I wish canned crushed tomatoes actually had the texture of a hand-crushed tomato, but the consistency is usually smooth like that of a puree, with just a small amount of texture. The flavor is a bit more "cooked" than that of canned whole tomatoes, but crushed tomatoes are fine for dishes that will be pureed anyway.

PUREE: Tomato puree is thicker and smoother than crushed tomatoes, giving the cook even less control over the final consistency of the dish.

SAUCE: Tomato sauce is very smooth and pourable, and it generally contains seasonings. Again, why bother?

PASTE: Thick, intensely flavored tomato paste is in its own category, as you use it more as an accent than a main ingredient. It comes in 6-ounce (170 g) cans, which can be problematic because you rarely use that amount for one recipe, leaving you with a partially used can that might easily get lost and moldy in the wilds of the back of your refrigerator. But tomato paste freezes well (as do all tomato products), so you can pop the excess into a freezer bag. If you're feeling organized, go ahead and spoon tablespoon-size portions onto a piece of parchment, freeze them, and then, once frozen, pop them into freezer bags, making it easy to retrieve the measured amount that you need for a recipe. A simpler solution is to buy tomato paste in a tube. You use what you need, and the tube keeps the rest fresh in the refrigerator.

THE INSIDER'S CANNED TOMATO

Forget the ballyhoo around San Marzanos—for me, the real prize is an under-the-radar, meant-for-food-service canned tomato from a family-owned tomato cannery in Modesto, California. I learned about Stanislaus from a chef friend, and now I spy their cans in pro kitchens around the country. Alta Cucina is the name of the variety I use. Small, fully ripe, tender, and sweet, with no stringiness or unripe cores, these tomatoes are so good that you could simply crush them and add a bit of salt and olive oil and you'd have a gorgeous pasta sauce or pizza topping.

Stanislaus doesn't sell at retail or direct to consumers, but I've bought their tomatoes from WebstaurantStore.com, which sells to consumers as well as food service, and they are also available through Amazon. The downside is that the only size is a 6-pound 7-ounce (2.92 kg) can, but the upside is that they are a fantastic value at about $1.00 per pound (450 g), especially when compared with DOP San Marzanos, which clock in at closer to $3.50 per pound (450 g) at retail. I simply measure out what I need and freeze the rest . . . and often use the cheerful cans to hold seeds and other gardening paraphernalia.

Tomato Snacks and Drinks

Grilled Bread with Tomato and Olive Oil

Spanish pan con tomate is one of those dead-simple dishes in which a small handful of basic ingredients creates a symphony of satisfaction. In the classic, the diner rubs a piece of grilled bread with a clove of garlic and the cut face of a half tomato until the bread has soaked up the tomato goodness. This version is a bit easier to manage, plus the tiny bowls of tomato puree look so pretty on the table.

As with any dish with few ingredients, each one needs to be excellent. Ripe tomatoes go without saying, as does good olive oil (see page 15). The only tricky part is the bread. You need a well-made loaf that has an open crumb structure, with little pockets for the tomato juices and pulp to tuck into—perhaps something like a ciabatta. You can grill the bread on a grill, under the broiler, or in a grill pan on the stovetop.

SERVES 4 AS AN APPETIZER

2 large very ripe tomatoes (or the equivalent amount of smaller tomatoes)

Flaky salt or kosher salt

Sherry vinegar (optional)

Sugar (optional)

Four ¾-inch (2 cm) slices good bread (see headnote)

Extra-virgin olive oil

2 garlic cloves, halved

Bring a medium pot of water to a boil. Cut out the cores from the tomatoes and cut an X in the skin at the opposite end. Drop the tomatoes into the boiling water and boil for a few seconds, until you see the skins peeling back around the X. With a really ripe tomato, this will happen quickly.

Scoop out the tomatoes and rinse under cool water, then leave until cool. Note: You usually see instructions to plunge the tomatoes into ice water after boiling to stop them from cooking further, but I don't think we need to do that here. I want the flesh to soften a bit, so I don't mind some carryover cooking. And setting up an ice bath is a (minor) pain.

Peel off the skin, cut the tomatoes in half through the equator, and grate on the large holes of a box grater into a bowl. (Alternatively, pulse the tomatoes in a food processor, but I like to keep a bit of texture.) Taste the tomato puree, and if it's perfect, leave as is; otherwise, season lightly with salt and a few drops of sherry vinegar. And if your tomato is acidic, no shame in adding a pinch of sugar. Set aside.

Grill the bread until it's crisped overall and the edges are quite dark—a little carbon flavor is good. Brush the grilled bread on one side with olive oil while it's still hot, and then rub a cut garlic half over the surface of each slice, just enough to transfer some flavor but not so much that you use up the whole half clove—unless the garlic is beautifully fresh and you love garlic. If your slices of bread are large, cut them in half.

Sprinkle the grilled bread with flaky salt. Serve while still warm with a little bowl of tomato puree and a spoon for each diner.

Fresh Tomato Salsa
That Clings to the Chip

While chips and salsa of any kind are always welcome at my table (and occasionally constitute dinner), I'm not a fan of the type of salsa in which all the ingredients are raw. Fresh tasting, yes, but those pico de gallo–style salsas are impossible to keep on the chip! I want the flavor of ripe, fresh tomatoes, but with a slightly sloppier, clingier consistency.

This salsa has the perfect balance with garlic, onion, and chiles taking a trip through the sauté pan before being combined with finely chopped fresh tomatoes that have been allowed to drain. The tomato juice gets added to the sauté pan with the aromatics, so no flavor is lost.

I usually chop the ingredients by hand, but a food processor is a perfectly fine way to hasten the task of chopping the onion, chiles, and garlic. Just please don't chop the tomatoes in the processor, as it aerates them and makes them sort of pink and foamy. I use three types of chile here to create layers of flavor, but use what you like, adding more jalapeño if you like chile heat. I don't, so this amount is for a mild-ish salsa.

And think outside the chip bowl: this salsa is also perfect for dipping vegetables into, as a topping for grilled fish or chicken, or as a condiment to swirl into a pot of beans. (Pictured on page 36)

MAKES 3 CUPS (650 G)

1½ pounds (650 g) tomatoes (not Romas or other paste type)

Kosher salt

Extra-virgin olive oil or vegetable oil

½ cup (75 g) finely diced onion

½ cup (90 g) finely chopped seeded fresh mild green chile, such as Anaheim or Hatch

½ cup (90 g) finely chopped seeded fresh poblano chile

1 small (25 g) fresh hot green chile, such as jalapeño, seeded and finely chopped

Core the tomatoes, cut them in half through the equator, and gently squeeze the seeds into a fine-mesh sieve set over a bowl. Press the seeds with a rubber spatula or the back of a spoon to push the juices into the bowl, then discard the seeds. The juicy gel around the seeds is very high in glutamic acid and, hence, super tasty (see page 13). Keep the sieve over the bowl.

Slice the tomato halves very thinly, then cut the slices into very small dice; aim for ¼ inch (6 mm) or smaller. Chop again so you have very fine tomato bits. Scoop them and all the juices that are now on your cutting board into the sieve over the bowl. Stir in about ½ teaspoon salt and let drain for about 20 minutes while you prepare the other ingredients.

In a large skillet, heat a glug of olive oil over medium-high heat. Add the onion, all three chiles, and a pinch of salt. Cook, stirring, until the vegetables begin to sizzle gently, then reduce the heat and keep cooking, stirring often, until the onion is soft and fragrant but not actually browned, 3 to 4 minutes.

2 or 3 garlic cloves, finely chopped

1 teaspoon ground cumin, plus more to taste

½ cup (15 g) chopped fresh cilantro leaves and tender stems

Fresh lime juice

Tortilla chips or sliced vegetables, for serving

Add the garlic and cumin and cook for another minute or so to soften—but not brown—the garlic. Pour the tomato juices from the bowl into the skillet, increase the heat a bit, and cook until the tomato juice has reduced and the onion-chile mixture is coated in syrupy tomato juice.

Scrape the mixture into a large bowl and let cool to room temperature, then stir in the tomatoes, cilantro, and a big squeeze of lime juice. Taste and adjust with more lime, salt, or cumin as necessary. Let the salsa sit for about 1 hour, if you have the time, so the flavors meld.

The salsa will stay nice in the fridge for up to 3 days.

Fresh Tomato Salsa
That Clings to the
Chip (page 34)

Upgraded Chile
con Queso Dip
(page 39)

Roasted Green
Tomato Salsa
(page 38)

Roasted Green Tomato Salsa

I suppose if you lived in the Garden of Eden, all your tomatoes would ripen, but for those of us in the real world, especially the Inland Northwest where I live (eastern Washington, just a short hop from the Canadian border), unripe tomatoes are a fact of life. I've learned to think of them not as a dream unfulfilled but rather as a distinctive ingredient with its own identity, like a tomato but different.

The main difference is the tarter flavor, since an immature tomato hasn't developed a lot of sugar. You can counter the sourness by roasting not only the tomatoes but also the other ingredients here to increase their sweetness and add a kiss of smoke and char.

Eat this salsa with chips, or try smothering a burrito or enchiladas with it or stirring it into a pot of beans. Or spread it over firm white fish fillets, such as cod or halibut, top with a chunk of butter, and roast in a hot oven. Note: I don't like a lot of chile heat, so this version would be characterized as "medium." For more chile heat, increase the jalapeños and/or add some killer hot sauce. (Pictured on page 37)

MAKES ABOUT 1½ CUPS (300 G)

2 or 3 jalapeños or other small fresh hot green chiles, seeded and cut into large chunks

1 or 2 Anaheim or other large fresh mild green chiles, seeded and cut into big chunks

1 small yellow or sweet onion, thickly sliced

3 garlic cloves, smashed

½ pound (225 g) green (unripe) tomatoes, cored and halved

Extra-virgin olive oil

Kosher salt and freshly ground black pepper

1 teaspoon ground cumin, plus more to taste

½ teaspoon ground coriander, plus more to taste

1 cup (30 g) lightly packed mixed tender fresh herbs (such as cilantro, flat-leaf parsley, mint, dill, chervil, and/or basil), roughly chopped

2 tablespoons fresh lime juice, plus more to taste

Preheat the oven to 425°F (220°C).

In a large bowl, combine the jalapeños, Anaheims, onion, garlic, and green tomatoes. Drizzle on a fair amount of olive oil, season lightly with salt and black pepper, and spread onto a sheet pan. Use two sheet pans if necessary to avoid crowding, or the vegetables will steam more than roast and brown.

Roast, turning the vegetables over with a spatula a couple of times during the process, until everything has collapsed and is starting to brown around the edges but is still juicy, 15 to 25 minutes. Remove from the oven, sprinkle on the cumin and coriander, and let cool on the pan(s).

Scrape the cooled vegetables into a food processor and pulse to create a chunky puree. Add the herbs and pulse a few more times to chop them up; a few larger leaves are fine.

Transfer to a smaller bowl and stir in the lime juice. Taste and add more salt, lime juice, cumin, and/or coriander to dial in the flavors. Be liberal with the salt, because it will temper the acidity of the green tomatoes.

Let the salsa rest for about 20 minutes before serving, if there's time, so the flavors meld. Store in the fridge and use within a couple of days.

Upgraded Chile con Queso Dip

I've got a soft spot for junk food that involves melted cheese of any kind. The type of chile con queso you get in a jar or from a generic Tex-Mex place is the pinnacle, and it seems to have the miraculous power to cure a hangover. I've tried making "gourmet" chile con queso with real cheese rather than Velveeta, but it misses the mark. I have, however, devised a way to elevate the guilty-pleasure dip to something with at least a touch of nutritional value—along with great flavor—by using fresh chiles and, of course, adding tomatoes. (Pictured on page 36)

MAKES ABOUT 3 CUPS (720 G)

Extra-virgin olive oil

¾ cup (150 g) diced fresh mild or medium-hot green chile, such as Hatch, Anaheim, or poblano

1 jalapeño or other fresh hot chile, seeded and minced

2 cups (225 g) diced tomatoes

12 ounces (340 g) Velveeta cheese, cut into chunks

¼ cup (7 g) finely chopped fresh cilantro

Tortilla chips, for serving

In a heavy-bottomed saucepan, heat a small amount of olive oil over medium heat. Add the chiles and cook for a few minutes to slightly soften. Add all but about ½ cup (50 g) of the tomatoes (set those aside) and continue to cook until the tomatoes are juicy and slightly softened but not turning into sauce, another 2 to 3 minutes.

Add the Velveeta and stir until it is melted and all the ingredients are blended and creamy. Stir in about half the cilantro. Put the dip into a serving dish and scatter the reserved tomatoes and cilantro over the top. Serve warm with chips.

Or Try This Idea

Substitute about 1 cup (250 g) Blasted Cherry Tomatoes (page 151) for the diced fresh tomatoes.

Quick-Pickled Cherry Tomatoes

Nothing makes you feel more "modern homesteader" than seeing a row of cheerful pickled veg lined up on your counter, and cherry tomatoes are a perfect candidate for this treatment. Pickled tomatoes make a great addition to a cheese board or as a snack on their own, and when chopped, they are wonderful on nachos and in potato salads, salsas, and mayonnaises. And a skewered pickled cherry tomato makes a fine garnish to an "Improved" Bloody Mary (page 66).

The easiest method of pickling is making refrigerator or quick pickles, meaning the produce is preserved in a mixture of vinegar, salt, and, usually, sugar, but no actual fermentation takes place. You get a supremely tangy result, and it's easy to add all sorts of flavorings. A true fermented pickle, such as a traditional dill pickle or Lacto-Fermented Pickled Tomatoes (page 42), relies on fermentation that takes place in the jar over several days.

You'll be diluting your vinegar with an equal amount of water, but the vinegar's flavor will still be part of your pickle flavor, so decide what will work best for you. I mostly use a not-too-expensive white wine vinegar or apple cider vinegar, but some people like mild rice vinegar or even the harsher, bracing distilled white vinegar. For a refrigerator pickle, the acid percentage in the vinegar isn't important, but if you plan to process and shelf-store your pickled tomatoes, be sure to use vinegar that's at least 5% acetic acid.

You don't need "pickling salt" per se, but don't use salt that has additives, such as iodized salt or salt that contains anticaking additives. Check the label. It's not super important, but some additives can cloud the pickling liquid.

Quick pickles last about 2 months in the refrigerator. To keep your pickles for a longer time, you'll need to process them in a boiling-water bath. With long unrefrigerated storage comes some risks, so if you go that route, please consult a good preserving guide, such as the *Ball Blue Book Guide to Preserving* (see Resources, page 239), which has been published for decades by the company that makes Ball canning jars.

MAKES 1 QUART (1 L)

About 1 pound (450 g) cherry tomatoes, rinsed, any stems removed

1 cup (240 ml) white wine vinegar

1 cup (240 ml) water

2 tablespoons sugar

1 tablespoon kosher salt

10 black peppercorns

1 cinnamon stick

1 medium dried red chile (such as cayenne or de árbol)

3 or 4 whole cloves

1 or 2 big strips lemon zest

NOTE

If you have hard water (contains lots of minerals, leaves spots on your glasses), you should use distilled water to avoid any possible discoloration of your pickle.

Poke each tomato with a skewer or toothpick to allow the pickling liquid to penetrate it easily, and drop into a sterilized 1-quart (1 L) canning jar or other container with a tight lid.

In a medium saucepan, combine the vinegar, water, sugar, salt, peppercorns, cinnamon, chile, cloves, and lemon zest and bring to a boil. Take the brine from the heat and let it cool a few degrees (so that you don't actually cook the tomatoes when you add the brine).

Pour the hot brine into the tomato jar, making sure all the flavorings make it into the jar as well and that all the tomatoes are submerged in brine. Seal, let the tomatoes cool to room temperature, and then refrigerate. Ideally, wait at least 1 week before serving so the tomatoes have time to absorb the brine. The tomatoes will be good in the fridge for up to 2 months.

Lacto-Fermented Pickled Tomatoes

This type of pickled tomato is actually fermented, not simply soured and preserved with vinegar and the cold of the refrigerator. It's just as easy to make as a refrigerator pickle, but it may require more judgment and attention on your part. Because you're not adding vinegar, all the preserving power will come from the lactic acid that develops naturally over a few days.

This recipe is inspired by *The Noma Guide to Fermentation* by René Redzepi and David Zilber, but lacto-fermenting vegetables is as old as humans, probably. All it requires is salt and some time. If you're familiar with sauerkraut, you're familiar with lacto-fermented vegetables.

The most common lacto-fermented tomato is probably the style made in Russia and other Eastern European cuisines, for which there seem to be as many recipes as there are babushkas. Some people don't add much beyond the tomatoes, perhaps some dill and black peppercorns, while others add plenty of herbs and spices, along with other vegetables, especially celery, chiles, or cucumbers. I like to stick to tomato as the main player but make the brine a bit complex with flavorings; once I've eaten the tomatoes, I drink the brine. A shot of ice-cold salty-sweet-sour-spiced brine on a hot summer day is an amazing tonic!

The fermentation happens thanks to natural organisms that are everywhere in our environment, so the goal is to encourage their growth while discouraging the growth of unwanted organisms. It's pretty easy to manage this by sterilizing your jar or crock, washing your hands before you make the pickle, and *not* washing the tomatoes, at least not much. Ideally you're using home-grown or local market-grown organic tomatoes, so all you need to do is give them a light rinse to remove any surface dust.

MAKES 1 QUART (1 L)

About 1¼ pounds (565 g) tomatoes, or as many as will fit in a 1-quart (1 L) jar without packing them super tightly, leaving at least 1 inch (2.5 cm) of headroom

A few sprigs fresh dill, rinsed

6 to 10 garlic cloves, sliced (don't use prepeeled garlic in jars)

1 teaspoon black peppercorns

1 or 2 bay leaves

1 small dried red chile, such as cayenne or de árbol

NOTES

- Some tomatoes from the grocery store are coated in a light wax, which seems like it would interfere with fermentation, so I would not advise using commercially raised tomatoes.

- It's critical to measure your salt correctly, because you need enough to discourage unwanted bacteria but not so much that it impedes the development of lactobacillus—the "good" bacteria.

- You leave the tomatoes in the brine at room temperature with the top of the jar only lightly screwed on in order for fermentation gases to escape. The fermentation should begin after 3 or 4 days, depending on room temperature and the particular microflora on your tomatoes, so you'll want to begin close observation at Day Two. You want enough fermentation to make the tomatoes lightly tangy with perhaps the slightest bit of pétillance (fizz) but not so much that they become overly sour and mushy. You then stop the fermentation by transferring the pickles to the refrigerator, where they will continue to only slowly ferment.

2 cups (480 ml) water

1 slightly rounded tablespoon
(9 g) kosher salt (with no
additives) or pickling salt

2 tablespoons sugar

- One thing to look out for is a whitish substance called kahm yeast that often forms around lacto-fermenting fruit and vegetables. Though kahm yeast is totally harmless and tasteless, you don't want to encourage its growth. Spoon it off as soon as you see any developing.

- It's very important that your tomatoes and flavorings be totally submerged in the brine to avoid developing unwelcome molds, so leave some headroom and be sure the brine covers them by at least ½ inch (1.25 cm).

Sterilize a 1-quart (1 L) jar and lid by boiling them for 10 minutes (or check your dishwasher—some have a sterilizing mode).

Gently rinse your tomatoes and cut away any blemishes. Halve or quarter large tomatoes so they will fit into the jar.

Fill the jar with the tomatoes, leaving at least 1 inch (2.5 cm) of space at the top to allow the brine to totally cover the tomatoes. Add the dill, garlic, peppercorns, bay leaves, and chile, letting them tumble around the tomatoes a bit.

In a small saucepan, bring the water, salt, and sugar to a boil, swirling the pan to dissolve the salt and sugar. Don't let the water boil for more than a few seconds, or you will change the concentration of salt in the brine. Let the brine cool a few degrees and then carefully pour over the tomatoes. Screw the lid on very lightly and find an out-of-the-way place for them to rest for a few days, out of direct sunlight and not near a heat source (like your oven).

Let the tomatoes rest for 48 hours and then start testing. They probably will not be very fermented yet, but this will give you a baseline from which to evaluate the "doneness" as they develop.

First, look for some fizz in the brine. Next, open the lid and sniff—do you get a sour, vinegary but pleasant smell? Once you detect bubbles and a nice pickle-y aroma, which might take a few days, use a sterile utensil to lift out a tomato to taste. You're looking for lightly soured, complex, fermented flavor. (Don't put the part you bit back in the jar.)

Once you've gotten to a good level of fermentation, screw on the lid (but not too tightly) and store the tomatoes in the refrigerator. They will continue to slowly ferment, so at some point they may become too sour for you. But you probably will have eaten them all before then and will be ready to make the next batch!

Tomato Toasts with Toppings

Whether you call them crostini, bruschetta, or toasts with toppings, the idea is the same: a small slice of grilled bread that's topped with something wonderful and served as a snack or first course. And what could be more wonderful than tomatoes in any form, which will bring jewel colors and lots of sweet-tangy juices to soak into the bread.

This type of snack is always a brilliant addition to an appetizer spread—easy to make, inexpensive, and substantial enough to keep the wine or cocktails in balance. And toasts with toppings are a good mix-and-match opportunity, allowing you to create variety on the table with a few basics (bread and tomatoes) along with accents from whatever herbs and condiments you have on hand.

Following is a method without specific quantities of ingredient, because it's all about what works with your size and shape of bread. Remember that you will need quite a bit of olive oil.

TO PREPARE THE TOASTS: The shapes you cut will depend on the shape of your loaf, the goal being to create a toast that has enough non-crust surface area to hold the toppings (and to have a nice crumb-to-crust ratio) but is still easy to pick up and eat with your hands (though I'll often set out knives and forks).

- Baguette shape—Cut at a sharp angle to create long, thin pieces.

- Boule shape—Cut slices into halves or quarters.

- Ciabatta or focaccia—Cut slices crosswise into halves.

Toast the bread before you oil it, to avoid burning the lovely olive oil. Grill, broil, or cook on a stovetop grill pan until the bread is nicely crisped overall and the edges are quite dark—a little carbon flavor is good—but not grilled mercilessly to the point where it's painful to crunch. Brush the grilled bread generously on one side with olive oil while it's still hot, and if you'd like a hint of garlic, rub the toasts with a cut clove of garlic. Then apply toppings and serve.

Toppings

- Blasted Cherry Tomatoes (page 151), burrata, fresh or dried mint, a few drops of balsamic vinegar.

- Classic Roasted Tomatoes (page 48) or Cherry Tomato Confit (page 231) and anchovy-Parmigiano butter. To make the flavored butter, chop a few anchovy fillets and mash them into slightly softened butter, along with a healthy amount of grated Parmigiano-Reggiano, some grated lemon zest, salt, and black pepper. Spread the butter onto the toasts while it's warm but not hot, so it melts but doesn't totally disappear.

- Ricotta lightly seasoned with curry powder, halved or quartered fresh cherry tomatoes (cut them however you need to make them bite-size for easy eating), fresh or lightly sautéed corn kernels, chopped fresh chives or cilantro.

- A thin layer of Tomato Jam #2 (page 57), topped with thin slices of prosciutto.

CLASSIC ROASTED TOMATOES

There are so many ways to roast a tomato, from low and slow to blasting at high heat, and I use all the methods depending on my mood, my tomatoes, and the envisioned end use. By October, my freezer is always loaded with bags of roasted tomatoes of various types, ready to pull out and transform into a soup, stew, sauce, or braising liquid, or, for the ones that hold their shape nicely, to thaw and serve as a side dish. (Warm them gently in the oven and refresh with olive oil and flaky salt.)

This roasting method, however, is my favorite and also the one that I find the most unpredictable. When all goes right, the tomatoes have retained their half-tomato shape but have been reduced into a concentrated form of their raw selves. The edges are deeply caramelized, the centers are still moist, and the seeds sort of melt into the whole thing, becoming texture rather than an annoyance.

During roasting, in the ideal scenario, the tomatoes throw off copious juices, which you can pour off mid-roast and reduce on the stovetop into a savory-sweet syrup. However, every batch of tomatoes is different depending on the nature of the tomatoes. Super-juicy ones can end up collapsing into a smear rather than tender little pucks, and dry ones never quite transform; the process requires a measure of faith.

I'm describing what can go wrong not to discourage you from trying these, but rather to alert you to the variables you'll need to address along the way. After all, what is cooking if not managing variables as we guide ingredients through transformation into a desired and delicious outcome?

Managing the Variables

If you have tomatoes on the same pan that range in size from golf ball to tennis ball, the variations in size and fleshiness make it tricky to cook them evenly. Ideally, fill each sheet pan with the same type of tomato, or at least do a half-and-half pan. A medium tomato such as Early Girl works well roasted, juicy enough to develop flavor but not so juicy and fleshy that it "stews" and falls apart.

Some cooks scoop out the seed pockets before roasting, but I usually leave everything intact except any large stem ends; the seeds and juicy gel are the source of deep flavor (see page 13). I don't bother cutting out tiny stem nubs, as they soften and sort of disappear during cooking.

How many and which seasonings you add is up to you, but keep in mind the final destination. You may want to load up a few batches with Italian-leaning flavorings, knowing you'll use those tomatoes in a pasta sauce or on pizza, and also make some batches with just salt, to use in a dish with another palette of flavors. I'm all for piling on the rosemary, oregano, thyme, marjoram . . . any fresh herb that can withstand a long roasting. Don't use tender herbs such as basil or mint, because they just blacken and get bitter. I also don't use sage, because it is super strong, but it would work as long as you use restraint.

The main variable is the amount of juice. Too much, and your tomatoes will stew rather than roast; plus, the juices will overflow and cause a big mess. Too little juice, and they will burn on the pan, depriving you of a lovely roasted tomato syrup. But, more critically, the burnt juices

can cause the tomatoes themselves to burn and stick to the pan, introducing a bitter note to your batch.

Be sure to use a sheet pan (the type with a rim), because you will be dealing with some amount of juices. But the low rim of a sheet pan is better than the 2- or 3-inch (5 or 7.5 cm) walls of an actual roasting pan. You need enough exposure and airflow so the tomatoes roast rather than stew in liquid that can't evaporate. So use a sheet pan that measures about 13 by 18 inches (33 by 46 cm)—what a restaurant would call a half-sheet pan—and the heavier the better. Many cooks line their pans with parchment for easier cleanup, but I find that the juices sneak under the parchment anyway, and the parchment can get in the way of spooning off juices mid-roasting, so go with an unlined pan. Even if the juices burn, they soak off easily.

Make sure your oven rack is level so you don't have juices running to one side; if your rack is slanted, rotate your pan a few times during cooking, or, if things are super tilty, make a shim from foil to level things up.

Roasting time will depend on how the tomatoes respond to heat, but most medium tomatoes of medium juiciness will take about 2 hours at 350°F (180°C) to become the intensely sweet-tangy, slightly smoky, tender chewy disks we crave.

Almost any result will be delicious as long as the tomatoes aren't burnt, so be vigilant, and if you're planning to roast many pounds, cook a test batch to dial in the time and temperature before you commit your whole crop.

CLASSIC ROASTED TOMATOES

MAKES A BIT LESS THAN 1 POUND (450 G)

3 pounds (1.35 kg) smallish round tomatoes, such as Early Girl

Extra-virgin olive oil

1 teaspoon fresh thyme leaves

1 teaspoon chopped fresh rosemary

Kosher salt and freshly ground black pepper

Preheat the oven to 350°F (180°C).

Cut out the tomato stems, halve the tomatoes through the equator, and arrange cut side up on a sheet pan. Drizzle generously with olive oil, then sprinkle with the thyme, rosemary, and a light seasoning of salt and pepper.

Roast in the oven until the tomatoes have shrunk in size by at least half and are very shriveled, browned around the edges, and concentrated in flavor. Depending on the moisture content of your tomatoes, this could take from 1½ hours to 3 hours. If your tomatoes are giving off quantities of juice, pour it off to use as tomato syrup (see page 71).

Leave the roasted tomatoes on the sheet pan to cool. They'll be less fragile and easier to handle once they're cool. Transfer to an airtight container, slightly shingled in flat rows so they don't get crushed, and store in the refrigerator for up to 3 days or freeze in zip-top freezer bags or a freezer-safe container for up to 3 months.

Good Things to Do with Classic Roasted Tomatoes

Serve on their own as a side dish; blend into mayonnaise or ricotta; chop and fold into cooked grains or beans; top crostini or puff pastry (see page 226) as an appetizer; toss with pasta, Italian sausage, and broccoli rabe.

Grilled Cheese with Sun-Dried Tomato and Smoky Red Pepper Mayonnaise

It's hard to imagine improving on a classic grilled cheese sandwich, but spreading the bread with mayonnaise that's flavored with sun-dried tomatoes and roasted red peppers certainly elevates the situation. This makes a rich sandwich, so choose a bread that can handle a bit of fat without getting too soggy, such as a whole-grain or sourdough loaf.

MAKES 1 SANDWICH

2 slices good-quality bread (if the crusts are tough, trim them off, just like Mom did)

About 2 tablespoons Sun-Dried Tomato and Smoky Red Pepper Mayonnaise (page 52)

A few slices sharp cheddar, American, or other cheese that you like in a grilled cheese sandwich

Butter

Spread one side of each slice of bread with the mayonnaise, taking care to get it all the way to the edges. You may need more or less than 2 tablespoons, depending on the surface area of your bread.

Arrange the cheese on one slice of bread, then put the two slices together. Set a skillet that's the right size for your bread (too large, and you'll end up with burned butter) over medium-high heat, add about 1 tablespoon (15 g) butter, and swirl it around to coat the skillet; as soon as it stops foaming, lay your sandwich in the skillet. Turn the heat down to medium-low and fry the sandwich slowly until the first side is deep golden brown and you can see that the cheese is beginning to melt.

Transfer the sandwich to a plate and wipe out any burned butter. Increase the heat back to medium-high and add another bit of butter, and as soon as it stops foaming, add the sandwich back on the uncooked side. Cook until the second side is lovely and toasty and the cheese looks melted.

Transfer to a cutting board, cut in half, and serve right away.

Or Try This Idea

Spread the bread with Tomato Jam #2 (page 57) instead of the mayonnaise.

Fried Green Tomatoes
with Three Sauces

The features that make green—as in unripe, not a green cultivar—tomatoes not great for eating raw in salads are what make them perfect for the frying pan: their firm texture means they hold up well during frying, and their tart flavor is a good foil for the crumb coating that gets crisp in hot fat. You could eat them with a simple accompaniment, such as a squeeze of lemon or some hot sauce, or make one (or all) of these mayo-based sauces as a rich but zingy accompaniment.

Many fried green tomato recipes call for coating the slices with cornmeal, but that creates a slightly gritty texture, so I use panko bread crumbs instead. They offer a crunchier, more delicate texture, and they absorb some of the tomato juice and cling nicely to the slices. The small amount of buttermilk in the egg dip does add some flavor, but don't go buy a carton just for this; plain milk works, too.

These are beautiful as a first course, or try them in a sandwich.

SERVES 2

2 large green (unripe) tomatoes, cored and cut into ½-inch (1.25 cm) slices

Kosher salt

1 cup (130 g) all-purpose flour

1 egg

1 tablespoon buttermilk or milk

2 cups (100 g) panko bread crumbs

Olive oil or vegetable oil, for shallow-frying

Flavored mayonnaise(s) of choice (recipes follow)

Or Try This Idea

Spread a hoagie-style roll with the mayo of your choice (or plain mayo) and layer on the fried tomatoes with sliced fresh mozzarella and a small handful of arugula.

Arrange the tomato slices on a cooling rack set over a sheet pan to catch the drips (if you don't have a rack, just spread out the slices on the sheet pan). Sprinkle lightly with salt and leave to drain for at least 20 minutes, and up to 1 hour.

Set up a frying station: Put the flour on a plate, beat the egg and buttermilk together in a shallow bowl, and spread the panko on another plate or in a shallow bowl (a pie pan is good for this). Set out a few paper towels on a tray on which to drain the fried slices.

Blot the tomatoes with paper towels.

Pour about ½ inch (1.25 cm) olive oil or other oil into a large skillet. Heat the oil over medium-high heat until quite hot but not smoking (365°F/185°C). Dredge a slice of tomato in flour, dip it in the egg on both sides, and then dredge it through the panko, patting to make sure you have a nice, even crust on both sides. Carefully place it in the hot oil and repeat with a few more slices. You don't want to crowd the pan, which would lower the oil temperature and ultimately make the crumb coating a bit greasy, so fry in batches as necessary.

Fry until the crumbs are golden brown and the tomatoes are heated through, about 3 minutes each side. If the crumbs seem to be browning too fast, reduce the heat a bit to allow them to toast and the tomato slice to heat through and soften slightly. Drain the fried tomatoes on the paper towels.

Serve while nice and hot, with a dollop (or three) of mayonnaise on the side.

continues

SUN-DRIED TOMATO AND SMOKY ROASTED RED PEPPER MAYONNAISE

MAKES ABOUT 1 CUP (225 G)

½ cup (125 g) mayonnaise, preferably Hellmann's or Best Foods

½ cup (125 g) chopped roasted red pepper (from a jar is fine)

¼ cup (30 g) chopped drained oil-packed sun-dried tomatoes

1 teaspoon sweet or hot smoked paprika, or more to taste

½ teaspoon kosher salt and many twists of freshly ground black pepper

1 teaspoon sherry vinegar, or more to taste

In a food processor, combine the mayonnaise, roasted red pepper, sun-dried tomatoes, smoked paprika, salt, black pepper, and vinegar and spin until nicely blended and mostly smooth (a little texture is nice). Taste and adjust the seasoning with more paprika, salt, black pepper, and/or vinegar to taste, if desired. Let the mayo sit for about 30 minutes before serving to allow the flavors to open up.

Taste and adjust the seasoning again right before serving. The mayo will keep in the refrigerator for up to 3 days.

SWEET ONION AND CURRY MAYONNAISE

MAKES ABOUT ¾ CUP (200 G)

1 tablespoon extra-virgin olive oil or vegetable oil

½ cup (75 g) finely chopped sweet onion, such as Vidalia or Walla Walla, or yellow onion

2 teaspoons finely chopped fresh ginger

Kosher salt

½ teaspoon ground turmeric

1½ teaspoons mild or hot curry powder

½ cup (125 g) mayonnaise, preferably Hellmann's or Best Foods

1 teaspoon fresh lime juice, plus more to taste

Hot sauce

In a small skillet, heat the oil over medium heat. Add the onion, ginger, and a generous pinch of salt. Cook, stirring frequently, until the onion is very soft, fragrant, and light golden brown, about 10 minutes; don't let them actually brown. Add the turmeric and curry powder and cook for another minute or so to bloom the spices; let cool.

In a small bowl, stir together the cooled onion, mayonnaise, lime juice, and a few shakes of hot sauce. Taste and adjust the seasoning with more salt, lime juice, and/or hot sauce. Let the mayo sit for about 30 minutes before serving to allow the flavors to open up.

Taste and adjust the seasoning again right before serving. The mayo will keep in the refrigerator for up to 3 days.

TRIPLE-LEMON MAYONNAISE

MAKES ABOUT ½ CUP (125 G)

½ cup (125 g) mayonnaise, preferably Hellmann's or Best Foods

2 tablespoons finely minced preserved lemon peel (if you can't get preserved lemon, increase the amount of lemon juice and zest, to taste)

1 teaspoon finely grated lemon zest

2 tablespoons fresh lemon juice, plus more to taste

¼ teaspoon sugar, plus more to taste

Kosher salt

Hot sauce

In a small bowl, stir together the mayonnaise, preserved lemon peel, lemon zest, lemon juice, sugar, and salt to taste. Taste and adjust the seasoning with more salt, sugar, or lemon juice, adding hot sauce to taste. Let the mayo sit for about 30 minutes before serving to allow the flavors to open up.

Taste and adjust the seasoning again right before serving. The mayo will keep in the refrigerator for up to 3 days.

Welsh Rarebit on Toast with Tomato Jam

Growing up, I had an aunt who was a very early proponent of "health food," bless her heart. When we would visit, my parents would stop the car at the end of my aunt and uncle's driveway and admonish us kids to eat everything we were served and that there would be no making of funny faces. One dish that stuck with me was "Welsh rarebit," which for my aunt was a thin orange liquid poured over a very dry rusk of some kind.

I needed a few decades of distance from that meal before I realized that Welsh rarebit was in fact exactly the kind of food I craved—whole-grain bread slathered with savory, bubbling cheese sauce seasoned with a bit of mustard and dark beer. True health food!

Here I've given it my own stamp with the addition of tomato: a slick of Tomato Jam #2 for a sweet-hot note. If you'd like to embellish further, see Or Try This Idea.

SERVES 4

3 tablespoons (45 g) butter

3 tablespoons all-purpose flour

⅔ cup (160 ml) stout, porter, or other dark beer or a dry hard cider

8 ounces (225 g) extra-sharp cheddar, grated

1 teaspoon mustard powder, such as Colman's

2 tablespoons Worcestershire sauce

Kosher salt and freshly ground black pepper

4 to 8 slices hearty artisan-style bread (not packaged sliced bread)

Tomato Jam #2 (page 57)

In a small saucepan, melt the butter over medium heat. Add the flour and whisk to form a smooth paste (called a roux). Cook for another minute or two, until the roux has lost its raw flour flavor, smells nutty, and is turning light gold.

Whisk in the stout and simmer until you have a slightly thickened sauce and most of the lumps are gone; the sauce will be thick and pasty at this point. Add the cheddar, mustard powder, and Worcestershire sauce and stir until the cheese has melted and the sauce looks smooth and creamy. Season lightly with salt and generously with black pepper. Taste and adjust the seasoning; set aside. (Note: The cheese sauce will last in the fridge for 3 days, so if you don't use it all in one sitting, save it for a quick snack later.)

Heat the broiler to high. Meanwhile, toast the bread lightly in a toaster or under the broiler. If using the broiler, toast one side a bit darker than the other.

Spread one side of each slice (the lighter side) with a thin layer of tomato jam. Arrange on a sheet pan jam side up. Spoon a generous layer of cheese sauce over everything and broil until the cheese is bubbling and browned. Serve right away.

Or Try This Idea

Before adding the cheese sauce, top the bread with a slice of fresh tomato, a few pieces of Low and Slow Roasted Plum Tomatoes (page 164), Classic Roasted Tomatoes (page 48), Cherry Tomato Confit (page 231), or one of the tomato pickles (see pages 40 and 42).

Tomato Jam #1— Citrus and Ginger

This jam is simple and sunshiney, thanks to three of my favorite ingredients: tomatoes, citrus, and ginger. You'll macerate the ingredients with the sugar for a few hours (up to overnight), a method I learned from reading Alsatian preserve maker Christine Ferber's wonderful book *Mes Confitures*. (By the way, don't peel the citrus.) Her method actually has you macerate them in the fridge overnight, then bring the ingredients to a boil and put them back in the fridge—sometimes a few cycles of this. I, of course, am too lazy for that, and I have found that one maceration period produces excellent results.

I love this jam spread on warm corn bread with butter, on toasted English muffins, and on crackers spread with fresh goat cheese.

MAKES 2 PINTS (900 G)

3 pounds (1.35 kg) tomatoes (a variety is nice, including some green/unripe tomatoes), cored and cut into chunks

1 large lemon or Meyer lemon, washed, thinly sliced, seeds flicked out, and slices cut into quarters

1 navel orange, washed, thinly sliced, seeds flicked out, and slices cut into quarters or eighths

1 tablespoon very finely chopped fresh ginger

3 cups (600 g) sugar, plus a bit more if you are using a lot of green (unripe) tomatoes

Pinch of kosher salt

NOTE

I don't use pectin in my jams, as many recipes do to ensure a firm enough set, because I like to let my jams be what they want to be. A little runny but with great flavor? Perfect.

In a large bowl, combine the tomatoes, lemon, orange, ginger, sugar, and salt. Toss to mix and let macerate for at least 2 hours, and up to overnight. (If you're going to leave the ingredients longer than 2 hours, put them in the refrigerator.)

Put the tomato-sugar mixture in a large deep skillet or a wide saucepan—or that cute copper jam pan you got as a wedding gift—and bring to a simmer, stirring and scraping the bottom of the pan so nothing burns.

Simmer everything, stirring frequently, until the tomatoes have broken down, the citrus slices are tender, and the jam is thick and glossy and reads at least 221°F (105°C) on a candy thermometer. To test another way: Slide your jam off the heat to pause the cooking while you test. Put a small plate in the freezer for a few minutes, then drizzle a spoonful of the jam on the cold plate and put it back in the freezer for a few minutes. Take it out, and if the jam is quite set up, it should be done. If it still seems runny, keep cooking for a few more minutes.

Put the jam into sterilized ½-pint (240 ml) jars (or whatever size you have) and either cool on the counter and store in the fridge for up to 1 month or process in a boiling-water bath for about 10 minutes (check a good reference such as the *Ball Blue Book Guide to Preserving* for details on this process); the processed jam will be safe to store in the cupboard for at least 6 months.

Tomato Jam #2—
Sweet and Spicy

Though still quite sweet, this jam leans toward savory, more like a chutney. You can improvise a bit with the spices if you don't have this exact lineup of ingredients, but be sure to use the ginger, onion, and chile. Adding some pomegranate molasses (also called pomegranate syrup) underscores the jam's sweet-tart balance, but if you don't have any, just use a bit more vinegar.

Spread a thin layer of jam on a ham and cheese sandwich or an egg-and-ham breakfast sandwich, serve a spoonful with grilled pork chops or sausages, or top some soft creamy cheese with a drizzle of jam and serve with crackers. (Pictured on page 30)

MAKES 1½ PINTS (700 G)

2¼ pounds (1 kg) tomatoes, cored and cut into chunks

2 cups (400 g) sugar

¼ cup (40 g) finely chopped onion

¼ cup (30 g) finely chopped fresh hot green chile, such as jalapeño

A 4-inch (10 cm) dried hot red chile, such as cayenne or de árbol

2 tablespoons very finely chopped fresh ginger

½ teaspoon kosher salt

½ teaspoon ground cinnamon

½ teaspoon Madras-style curry powder

¼ teaspoon ground cloves

¼ teaspoon ground coriander

¼ teaspoon ground cumin

2 tablespoons pomegranate molasses (optional)

1 tablespoon sherry vinegar or balsamic vinegar (use a bit more if not using the pomegranate molasses)

In a large bowl, toss together the tomatoes and sugar. Let macerate for at least 1 hour, and up to overnight. (If you're going to leave things longer than 2 hours, put them in the refrigerator.)

Put the tomatoes and sugar in a large deep skillet or a wide saucepan and bring to a simmer, stirring and scraping the bottom of the pan so nothing burns. Add the onion, fresh chile, dried chile, ginger, salt, cinnamon, curry powder, cloves, coriander, cumin, pomegranate molasses (if using), and vinegar.

Simmer everything, stirring frequently, until the jam is thick and glossy and reads at least 221°F (105°C) on a candy thermometer. To test another way: Slide your jam off the heat to pause the cooking while you test. Put a small plate in the freezer for a few minutes, then drizzle a spoonful of the jam on the cold plate and put it back in the freezer for a few minutes. Take it out, and if the jam is quite set up, it should be done. If it still seems runny, keep cooking for a few more minutes.

Taste the jam for seasoning, adjusting with more of any of the spices or salt, removing the dried chile. Put into sterilized ½-pint (240 ml) jars (or whatever size you have) and either cool on the counter and store in the fridge for up to 1 month or process in a boiling-water bath for about 10 minutes (check a good reference such as the *Ball Blue Book Guide to Preserving* for details on this process); the processed jam will be safe to store in the cupboard for at least 6 months.

Fried Tomato Leaves with Anchovies and Mozzarella

Admittedly, this is a bit of a "novelty" snack, something that is as much fun to serve and talk about as it is delicious to eat. And it *is* delicious! A riff on the Italian snack of an anchovy fillet sandwiched between sage leaves and fried, these little fritters are crisp and intensely salty, perfect to serve with an icy martini or Cosmato (see page 67). The fritters need to be eaten nice and hot, so prepare these while your guests mingle in the kitchen as you work—"from pan to hand." Only make fried tomato leaves if you have tender, smallish tomato leaves, as larger, more mature leaves will be too tough and chewy; read more about tomato leaves on page 61.

MAKES 1 "SANDWICH," OR AS MANY AS YOU LIKE

1 egg, beaten

Flour

Extra-virgin olive oil, for deep-frying

1 nice anchovy fillet, blotted dry

1 sliver fresh mozzarella or other cheese

2 tender tomato leaves of roughly the same size (about 3 inches/7.5 cm)

Small lemon wedge, for serving (optional)

Set up a frying station: Put the beaten egg on a small plate and the flour on another, and line a third plate with a paper towel.

Pour about 1 inch (2.5 cm) of olive oil into a deep saucepan (something that will contain the hot oil even if it bubbles up a bit) and heat to about 365°F (185°C).

Sandwich the anchovy fillet and the sliver of cheese between the tomato leaves so they line up nicely together, pressing them lightly to stick. Dip the leaf sandwich into the egg, making sure it's thoroughly coated in egg, and then dredge it thoroughly in the flour (your fingers will get messy, but you need to use them so you can pinch all the ingredients together).

Shake off excess flour and carefully slide the sandwich into the hot oil—stand back a bit as you do this, because the leaves will snap and sputter! Fry until golden brown on both sides, 1 to 1½ minutes total. Transfer to the paper towels to drain. Repeat with more leaves and filling.

Serve the tomato leaf sandwiches right away, while still hot, with a squeeze of lemon, if you like.

LET'S TALK ABOUT TOMATO LEAVES

Anyone who's grown a few tomato plants knows the haunting scent of the leaves. Related to the flavor of the tomatoes themselves, but not quite the same, the fragrance of a tomato leaf when crushed between your fingers is green, fresh, vegetal, slightly citrusy, maybe with a hint of cedar? Hard to describe, but you want to inhale it.

The scent is so intoxicating that you'll find high-end scented candle makers and even perfumers featuring tomato leaf scent in their products.

So tomato leaves smell good enough to eat . . . but can we? We eat the leaves attached to beets and turnips and carrots, so why not tomatoes? Until recently the common wisdom was that tomato leaves were toxic and should not be eaten. But, as we know, common wisdom isn't always wise. Tomatoes themselves were thought to be poisonous by British colonists for a couple of centuries.

Part of the confusion comes from the fact that the tomato—*Lycopersicon esculentum*—is part of the Solanaceae family, which includes deadly nightshades and other poisonous plants. Any adjacency to a plant called "deadly" can kill your appetite pretty quickly.

It was also common wisdom that tomato leaves contain solanine, a toxic alkaloid that we encounter in potatoes—that green layer that forms just under the skin when the potatoes have been exposed to too much sunlight and which we're advised to cut off and not eat.

Food scientist Harold McGee clarifies, however, that solanine is a potato alkaloid and tomato leaves have their own alkaloid called tomatine, which not only isn't toxic but is also potentially beneficial. According to some research, tomatine lowers LDL, the bad cholesterol, in animals. So those deer that marauded through your garden? Excellent cardiovascular health!

Paul Bertolli, an American chef who rose to prominence when he led the kitchen at Chez Panisse in the 1980s, published a tomato leaf sauce recipe that may be the first—possibly the only—widespread recipe that uses tomato leaves. I admire both Paul Bertolli and Harold McGee, so I started my own experiments with leaves.

There are two types of tomato leaf. The first type is the "regular" leaf, which can be dark or light, sturdy or wispy (actually "wispy droopy" is a technical descriptor), but is generally fairly delicate with deep fingerlike serrations along the edges. Regular leaves have two variants: rugose, which means the leaves are darker and puckered, a bit like those of Savoy spinach, and angora, which, like the sweater or bunny, is fuzzy. The second main category of tomato leaf is "potato leaf," which is broader, less serrated, and looks like, well, you guessed it. Potato leaf tomato leaves also can be rugose or angora (confused yet?).

The flavor of a tomato leaf is much like the fragrance: green, herbal, slightly lemony, and with a bitter edge, a bit like a chicory. You need to choose leaves that are fresh and tender, as more mature ones can be slightly dank-tasting. I've been eating only regular leaves that are not fuzzy or crinkled—*regular* regular leaves, if you will.

Even when you have young specimens, a sauce or salad made with only tomato leaves might be too intense, so pair them with other greens, as in Tomato Leaf, Arugula, and Other Mixed Greens Salad (page 77), in which the tomato leaves bring tart notes to the mix of greens. In Tomato Leaf and Basil Pesto (page 145), the grassiness of the leaves is balanced by sweet basil. Or use tomato leaves as you would any other leafy herb, cut in fine chiffonade and sprinkled on a pasta or salad.

Tomato Shrub

Shrub is an old-fashioned name for an old-fashioned concoction, originally made as a cold refreshing drink in hot Muslim countries (where it was called *sharbat*), then in many parts of the world as a way to preserve fresh fruits, especially berries. In eighteenth-century America, shrubs became popular beverages of fruit juice sweetened with sugar and soured with vinegar. In the last couple of decades, shrubs have become trendy again thanks to the convergence of the craft cocktail revival, the wellness movement (and the purported probiotic benefits of vinegar), and Western cooks' interest in Asian beverages such as Thai drinking vinegars.

Shrubs can be made a number of ways, but this one starts with tomato water, which I encourage you to always have on hand. You simply simmer tomato water with sugar and vinegar until everything's reduced to a bracing but enjoyable level of sweet-tart. Tomato shrub is delicious sipped on its own over ice, topped off with soda water or ginger beer (my favorite), or paired with other fruits and spices to make more complex soft and hard drinks (see the suggested flavor combinations in Shrub Sodas). Have fun experimenting!

MAKES ABOUT ¾ CUP (180 ML)

1 cup (240 ml) Tomato Water (page 70)

½ cup (100 g) sugar

½ cup (120 ml) white wine vinegar

In a small saucepan, simmer the tomato water, sugar, and vinegar over lowish heat until slightly syrupy and the flavor is balanced, about 30 minutes (you want an edge from the vinegar, but you don't want so much that your eyes water!). Cool and then store in the fridge for up to 2 weeks.

And Try These Ideas for Shrub Sodas

WATERMELON-TOMATO-LIME: Puree chunks of fresh watermelon, strain, and measure the volume. One pound (450 g) should give you about 1½ cups (360 ml) strained juice. Blend 2 parts watermelon juice to 1 part Tomato Shrub and add lime juice and a bit more sugar to taste. Add a little sparkling water for some fizz, if you like, and serve over ice.

TOMATO-PLUM-ROSEMARY: Plums often need a bit of encouragement to get their juices to flow, so here they need to be macerated first. Toss ½ pound (225 g) ripe plum chunks with the ½ cup sugar (100 g) in the Tomato Shrub recipe. Leave at room temperature for at least 20 minutes and up to a couple of hours, then transfer everything to a saucepan, add the rest of the tomato shrub ingredients, and simmer, pressing lightly on the plums, without mashing them into a puree, which would make your shrub cloudy. When the liquid looks syrupy (30 to 40 minutes, depending on juiciness of the plums), let cool, strain, and chill. Taste and add sugar to

taste, then add a little sparkling water for some fizz, if you like, and serve over ice, garnished with fresh mint.

TOMATO-GINGER-TURMERIC: Lightly smash 2 coin-size slices of fresh ginger and 1 slice of fresh turmeric root and add them to the ingredients for Tomato Shrub as you simmer everything. Once the mixture reaches a good syrupy consistency, taste it. If it's not spiced enough for you, leave the ginger and turmeric in the syrup as it cools and even when you store it. Once it's at a good level, remove the ginger and turmeric. Add a little sparkling water for some fizz, if you like, and serve over ice.

G & T & T (Gin & Tonic & Tomato)

My summer cocktail is a gin and tonic, and while I usually stick to the classic London dry–style gin, Fever-Tree tonic, and a big wedge of lime, I make an exception when I have tomato syrup in my fridge. The sweet-tart syrup rounds out the sharp edges of a citrus-only drink, and it also adds a lovely blush to a frost-kissed highball glass.

MAKES 1 COCKTAIL

Ice cubes

2 ounces (60 ml) Tomato Syrup (page 71)

2 ounces (60 ml) gin of your choice (Hendrick's is great in this drink)

Tonic water (Fever-Tree is excellent)

Slice of cucumber or lime wedge, for garnish

Fill a tall glass with ice cubes. Add the tomato syrup and then the gin, but don't stir. Float enough tonic water on top to fill the glass and add your garnish.

Serve the drink with a swizzle stick or straw so the drinker can blend the liquids before drinking, or give the drink a stir yourself once everyone has seen how pretty it is.

"Improved" Bloody Mary

In cocktail history, there was a period in the late nineteenth century when bartenders were expanding on what was then the only cocktail formula—spirits, sugar, bitters, and water or ice—by making drinks that included citrus or liqueurs. They called these more elaborate cocktails "improved," such as the Improved Brandy Cocktail.

I would never claim to have the skills of a true bartender (let alone "mixologist"), so my "improved" here is a bit tongue in cheek, but I really do prefer my version to the classic Bloody Mary. Because I use tomato syrup as the base, all the bracing fresh flavors are there, but gone is the thick canned tomato juice. A few drops of fish sauce stay subtle but boost the umami factor in this savory cocktail.

MAKES 1 COCKTAIL

½ cup (120 ml) Tomato Syrup (page 71)

1 teaspoon prepared horseradish

1 teaspoon fresh lemon juice

½ teaspoon Worcestershire sauce

¼ teaspoon fish sauce, preferably Red Boat (optional)

¼ teaspoon celery salt (optional)

Hot sauce

Kosher salt

Ice cubes

2 ounces (60 ml) vodka or other spirit of your choice

Garnishes aplenty: celery stick, spear of cucumber, olives on a skewer, lemon wedge, lime wedge, Quick-Pickled Cherry Tomatoes (page 40), Lacto-Fermented Pickled Tomatoes (page 42), peperoncini, chunk of pecorino cheese, and/or rolled-up slice of salami

In a mixing glass or other tall vessel, stir together the tomato syrup, horseradish, lemon juice, Worcestershire sauce, fish sauce (if using), celery salt (if using), a few dashes of hot sauce, and a pinch of salt. Taste and adjust with any of the ingredients to your liking.

Fill a tall glass with ice, add the vodka, and fill the glass with the Bloody Mary mix. Garnish at will!

Or Try This Idea

For a lighter drink, don't fill the glass all the way with Bloody Mary mix and spritz in a bit of sparkling water.

Cosmato

In case you don't get my bad pun of a title, this is a riff on a Cosmo (Cosmopolitan), the iconic cocktail of the 1990s that became a *Sex and the City* trope but is delicious when made well. A classic Cosmo consists of vodka, an orange liqueur such as Cointreau, cranberry juice cocktail (which is sweetened), and fresh lime juice. I think tomato with orange and lime sounds just as good or nicer than cranberry, so I use tomato syrup in its place.

MAKES 1 COCKTAIL

2 ounces (60 ml) vodka

1½ ounces (45 ml) Tomato Syrup (page 71)

¾ ounce (22 ml) fresh lime juice

½ ounce (15 ml) Cointreau or other triple sec orange liqueur

Sugar or simple syrup

Ice cubes

Neatly pared strip of tomato skin or 1 or 2 tiny cherry tomatoes on a toothpick, for garnish

Chill a cocktail glass, ideally a coupe or martini type, but any glass that will show off the gorgeous color will be fine.

Put the vodka, tomato syrup, lime juice, and Cointreau in a cocktail shaker. Taste and add a tiny bit of sugar or simple syrup to get a good balance of sweet-tart-bitter.

Fill the shaker with ice. Shake until icy cold (but don't shake so long that you dilute the cocktail too much) and strain into the chilled cocktail glass. Garnish and serve while the cocktail is still very cold and you're wearing Jimmy Choo stilettos. Just kidding.

TOMATO WATER AND TOMATO SYRUP

If you had asked me about tomato water a few years ago, before I started growing insane amounts of tomatoes in my garden, I would have said that tomato water was a rarefied substance that made sense at the French Laundry but not in a home kitchen. Too fussy, too expensive. Plus what would you do with it other than make gelée?

But once I found myself amassing bowls and baskets and apronfuls of ripe tomatoes that were begging for some kind of processing, I started to experiment with tomato water and, of course, totally changed my opinion. I now can say that tomato water is as valuable as good chicken stock in my kitchen and that, provided you have an inexpensive source of tomatoes, every cook should have a supply in their fridge or freezer.

Once you have tomato water, you're just about half an hour from tomato syrup. My first encounters with tomato syrup came even before I started experimenting with tomato water; the syrup was a by-product of roasting pounds of tomatoes from my garden. As the tomatoes roasted, they kicked off so much juice that it would have overflowed my sheet pan, so I was forced to pour it off a few times during cooking. I poured it into a saucepan and cooked it down just a bit more, until syrupy and sweet but still with tons of bright tomato flavor. Now it's definitely something I want to make purposefully, not just by accident.

Managing the Variables for Tomato Water

The process for making tomato water is simple: you chop or puree the tomatoes and then drain them in a fine mesh of some kind for several hours. The idea is to break down the cell walls of the tomatoes so they release the juice and leave the solids behind.

The easiest way is to blend the tomatoes in a blender or food processor, though I've made many batches just chopping the tomatoes by hand. Blend only until the tomatoes become a rough puree; blending for a long time to create a perfectly smooth consistency might chop open the seeds, which can add some bitterness; long blending also aerates the tomatoes, which seems to capture, rather than release, the juices.

In comparative tests, I found that the blender method yields about 30 percent more water than the hand-chop method, but it's good to know that you can make tomato water without electricity, in case you have the urge for a Bloody Mary when you're camping. That's not unreasonable.

I add a small amount of salt to the tomatoes, to encourage the juices to flow (salt draws out liquid from food via osmosis), but not so much that it makes the tomato water salty per se, as I like having a neutral juice that I can take in any direction, such as in a syrup to use as a sweet soda.

To drain the tomatoes, line a fine-mesh sieve with a double or triple layer of cheesecloth (most cheesecloth comes in lengths made up of several folds, so unfold once to get the width you need). You could use only the sieve, but more fine particles will slip through, making your tomato water pink and cloudy—not a big problem.

Set the sieve over a deep stainless steel bowl, add the cheesecloth, add the salted tomatoes, and then loosely cover the rig with a towel or plastic wrap, to keep the summer insect friends away. I usually start the process on the counter and eventually transfer it to the refrigerator if the weather is hot or I need to drain it overnight.

Stir the mixture from time to time, to make sure all the juices can flow through; the cheesecloth can get blocked by tomato solids. I find that you need to drain the tomatoes for at least 4 hours. Beyond that, the incremental amount of juice is small, but when time allows, I go for a longer drain. After all, tomato water is kind of precious.

The result from a drain through cheesecloth will be a light golden liquid with some fine peachy particles, which settle out as the water sits. For most purposes, having this lightly clouded tomato water is just fine—and I think the blush is gorgeous—but for some uses, such as for cocktails, a crystal-clear liquid is preferable. To get totally clear tomato water (which will retain a pale yellow or gold color), drain again through a coffee filter. Just note that this can take several hours.

TOMATO WATER

MAKES ABOUT 2 CUPS (480 ML)

2 pounds (900 g) very ripe and juicy
tomatoes (don't use plum tomatoes),
cored and roughly chopped

½ teaspoon kosher salt

Arrange a large fine-mesh sieve so it sits
securely over a bowl. Line the sieve with
a double or triple layer of cheesecloth
(moisten it and wring it out before lining
the sieve to prevent the cheesecloth from
floating around).

Put the tomatoes and salt in a blender
or food processor and blend until you
have a rough puree. Pour the tomatoes
into the sieve; if you have too many to fit,
wait until some of the juice has drained
and the tomato solids have collapsed
and then add the rest, or use two setups.

Loosely cover the tomatoes and leave
to drain for at least 4 hours, or up to
24 hours. Give the tomatoes a few gentle
stirs during the draining period, making
sure that the cheesecloth isn't clogged
with tomato solids.

You can squeeze the tomato solids to
get the last drops of liquid, but you risk
adding a lot of tomato particles to your
water, so if your goal is clarity, resist the
urge to squeeze.

If you want to repurpose the tomato
solids, freeze them and add them to a
batch of tomato soup, tomato paste, or
tomato sauce at your leisure. Otherwise,
add to your compost.

Store the tomato water in an airtight
container in the fridge, and use it within
5 days, or freeze for up to 2 months.

Good Things to Do with Tomato Water

Substitute for broth in risotto and other
rice dishes; use in minestrone-type soups;
enhance tomato sauces; use as a poaching
liquid for fish and shellfish; serve over ice as
juice.

Managing the Variables for Tomato Syrup

While a good output of tomato syrup can't be guaranteed when roasting tomatoes (see Classic Roasted Tomatoes, page 48), you can use a more straightforward method and simply reduce tomato water. If you start with 2 cups (480 ml) of tomato water, you will end up with ½ cup (120 ml) syrup that's a good, all-purpose consistency.

Use a small heavy-bottomed saucepan and a low simmer, which keeps the reduction process slow, allowing you to monitor the flavor and consistency so you can stop the syrup when it's just how you want it. Know that tomato water contains a lot of sugar, which will burn and get bitter if you let it cook down too much.

TOMATO SYRUP

MAKES ABOUT ½ CUP (120 ML)

2 cups (480 ml) Tomato Water (opposite)

Optional flavorings (see below)

In a small heavy-bottomed saucepan, bring the tomato water to a simmer over medium heat. Adjust the heat so the water simmers gently and cook until the tomato water has reduced by about three-quarters, or until you have the flavor and consistency you want. Some amount of tomato solids may accumulate around the edge of the pot, so for the clearest syrup, take care not to disturb them. Note that the syrup will thicken as it cools.

Pour into an airtight container and refrigerate for up to 5 days, or freeze for up to 2 months.

Flavorings for Tomato Syrup

Add one or a combination of these flavorful ingredients to the tomato water. Taste about halfway through the reduction process to check on the flavor; if it's pronounced, remove the flavorings. Otherwise, leave in

and strain out after the syrup is cooled and ready to use.

- 1 or 2 whole garlic cloves
- 2 or 3 slices fresh ginger
- A 4-inch (10 cm) piece fresh lemongrass, crushed
- 1 dried red chile, such as cayenne or de árbol
- ½ star anise
- 1 small cinnamon stick

Good Things to Do with Tomato Syrup

Make cocktails or sodas; whisk into vinaigrettes; glaze grilled fish, chicken, pork, or sausages; dress fruit salad, seafood salad, or ceviche.

Tomato Salads

A Perfect Platter of Sliced Tomatoes

When you are in possession of perfectly ripe tomatoes from your garden or local farm, your best move is to do almost nothing to them. Especially when the season is early and you're still marveling at the beauty and overall lusciousness of a tomato, a simple platter of sliced tomatoes will have a greater impact than any more involved preparation. (Pictured on page 73)

Even perfection can use a little fluffing, however, so here are a few tips for showcasing pristine summer tomatoes.

- USE A MIX OF COLORS AND SHAPES. And don't worry about creating organized rows on the platter. A more free-form organic look feels best to me.

- WARM THEM UP. If the tomatoes were in the refrigerator (see page 84), bring them to cool room temperature before serving for the best flavor and fragrance.

- SLICE THEM ON THE THICK SIDE. A thicker slice lets you experience the tomatoes' full juicy-satiny texture; I think ½ inch (1.25 cm) is good. Serve with a knife as well as a fork.

- SLICE YOUR TOMATOES RIGHT BEFORE SERVING. But if you do need to do so ahead of time, let the slices sit on a cooling rack set over a tray to catch the drips, so that too many juices don't pool on the platter. If your platter does look awash, spoon off some of the juices before serving.

- ADD A LIGHT SPRINKLING OF SALT, especially a flaky one. Salt brings out tomatoes' sweetness, but add it only at the last minute so the salt doesn't draw out the juices.

Okay, now let's get real. Unadorned perfect tomatoes are awesome, but after a few rounds of restrained simplicity in the beginning of the season, I want to start embellishing! Nothing to overwhelm the tomato, mind you, but tomatoes play so well with others, why not invite a few friends to the party?

- START WITH A THIN THREAD OF GOOD EXTRA-VIRGIN OLIVE OIL. My preference is an oil that's not super piquant, more on the fruity side. Some oils actually have tomato-leaf notes to their fragrance, including Italian oils from Nocellara or Cerasuola olives, but any good, fresh olive oil will do kind things for a ripe tomato.

- SHOWER THEM WITH HERBS. Fresh herbs are always appropriate, of course. Whole leaves look pretty but aren't always easy to eat, so tear or cut large leaves into smaller bits. Tender herbs such as basil, parsley, tarragon, cilantro, mint, chervil, chives, and dill are favorites. Or try shiso or its relative, perilla; both are in the mint family and have an intriguing spicy flavor that's lovely with sweet tomatoes. The flavor of hardier herbs such as rosemary, thyme, and oregano is delicious with tomatoes, but I don't like their tougher texture on raw tomatoes, so I usually save those herbs for cooked dishes.

- OR DELIVER THE HERBS IN THE FORM OF A PESTO. Double down on the tomato flavor and fragrance with a drizzle of Tomato Leaf and Basil Pesto (page 145), or try Parsley-Mint Pesto with Walnuts (page 175), or a classic basil pesto.

- ADD SOME ANCHOVIES, WHY NOT? Sprinkle chopped anchovy fillets over the tomato slices or lay a slender fillet on each slice. The umami flavors of each ingredient will reinforce that savory quality in each other.

- CREATE CONTRAST WITH BREAD CRUMBS. I mean homemade, crisped-in-olive-oil, nicely shaggy bread crumbs that keep their crunch even as they soak up some juices. (See Shaggy Bread Crumbs, page 78.)

- GO LARGE WITH CHEESE. Forget finely grated and use shards of Parmigiano-Reggiano, pecorino, or ricotta salata; crumbles or small chunks of feta; and, of course, fresh mozzarella, ideally pulled into small chunks rather than diced or sliced (see ideas for riffs on the classic mozz-tomato caprese salad, page 107).

- ADD A SALTY HIT. It always works to bring out the sweet-tangy notes in a tomato, so add a scattering of chopped (or whole) olives and/or capers.

- ADD SOME COMPLEXITY. Employ spices and seeds, such as a sprinkling of sour sumac or a shower of crunchy dukkah (a Middle Eastern mix of sesame seeds and nuts, usually with cumin and coriander seed) or za'atar (another popular Middle Eastern seasoning blend made from sesame seeds, oregano, thyme, sumac, and marjoram). To keep the seeds crunchy, don't add them until the last minute.

- DRIZZLE WITH CREAMY TAHINI DRESSING. Use good-quality tahini (I like Soom brand) thinned with some lemon juice and water and seasoned with salt and a little bit of grated garlic. A drizzle of tahini dressing with a sprinkling of za'atar would be a treat.

- OR DRIZZLE WITH A ZINGY VINAIGRETTE. A few spoonfuls of a vinegar- or citrus-based dressing will enhance the natural brightness of the tomatoes. See pages 94–95 for a few of my favorites.

Tomato Leaf, Arugula, and Other Mixed Greens Salad

I love the simplicity of a simple green salad served between dinner and dessert or as a fresh and fragrant companion to a simple lamb chop or piece of grilled fish, maybe with some nuts, bread crumbs, or cheese, but nothing else. Use a mix of sweet, tart, spicy, and bitter greens . . . the tomato leaves will add a bit of both tart and bitter. Choose only young, tender leaves, as mature ones can taste too much like eating, well, leaves (see page 61).

I like to keep my salad greens large and just fold them into convenient shapes and sizes with my knife and fork on the plate, but feel free to cut or tear the greens into smaller pieces—but not too small, or you'll lose all the leafy texture and visual appeal.

SERVES 4

A handful of tender tomato leaves (tart)

A handful of arugula (spicy)

1 head butter or Bibb lettuce (sweet)

½ small head radicchio or other fairly tender chicory (such as Treviso or Castelfranco) (bitter)

Fresh lemon juice

Extra-virgin olive oil

Kosher salt and freshly ground black pepper

Optional Add-Ins

½ cup (25 g) Shaggy Bread Crumbs (recipe follows)

1 cup (50 g) Parmigiano Croutons (recipe follows), crushed a bit if large

¼ cup (25 g) finely grated Parmigiano-Reggiano cheese

¼ cup (30 g) lightly toasted sliced almonds or pine nuts

Break or cut off any tough stems from the tomato leaves and arugula. Cut away the root end and core from the butter lettuce and separate the leaves, ripping the huge ones into smaller pieces. Cut the radicchio into ribbons ½ inch (1.25 cm) wide.

Wash and dry all the greens really well using a salad spinner, making sure you've spun off as much water as possible.

Pile the greens into a large salad bowl. Sprinkle on a couple of teaspoons of lemon juice and a couple of tablespoons of olive oil and toss to distribute. Season generously with salt and pepper and toss again.

Taste, and now dial in the seasoning with more lemon, oil, salt, and/or pepper. The salad should be savory and well dressed, but you should still taste the greens and feel their textures.

If using any of the add-ins, toss them in now. Serve the salad right away.

Or Try This Idea

Instead of dressing the salad with olive oil and lemon juice, use one of the vinaigrettes on pages 94–95. Or make a tomato syrup vinaigrette: Whisk 1 tablespoon Tomato Syrup (page 71) and 1 teaspoon sherry vinegar or good red wine vinegar with a generous pinch of salt and a few twists of freshly ground black pepper. Whisk in about 3 tablespoons good extra-virgin olive oil and a few basil leaves cut into fine ribbons. Taste and adjust so the seasoning level is balanced and bright.

continues

SHAGGY BREAD CRUMBS

Shaggy crumbs are an ideal finishing textural touch on almost any tomato salad, and they add a nice dimension to pastas as well. Make more than you think you'll need, because if you're like me, you will eat about 40 percent of the batch while it's still draining on the paper towel.

Obviously, the better the bread, the better the bread crumbs, but if you can't get your hands on a nice artisan loaf, you can make the crumbs with a packaged bread. Just tear the pieces a bit bigger, because they probably won't have as much crumb structure as artisan bread; hence they will collapse a bit as you fry them.

MAKES ABOUT 1 CUP (60 G)

Two ½-inch (1.25 cm) slices good-quality country-type bread (about 60 g total)

Extra-virgin olive oil

Kosher salt (optional)

If the crusts are tough, cut them off. Rip the bread into jagged pieces between ¼ and ½ inch (6 mm and 1.25 cm), trying not to compress the crumbs as you pinch and rip the bread.

Line a plate with paper towels. In a medium skillet, heat a generous glug of oil (about 2 tablespoons) over medium-high heat. You want enough oil so that all the crumbs will be lightly moistened. When you see the oil shimmering (but not smoking!), toss in a crumb. If it immediately sizzles nicely, add the rest. If it's quiet, wait until the oil heats a bit more.

Shake the pan and stir the crumbs so they all get coated with oil. Reduce the heat slightly so that the crumbs slowly brown and crisp, making sure to toss them around as they cook. You'll know they're getting close to done when the sound changes—you'll start to hear a rustling sound as the crumbs transform from soft to crisp. Pour the crumbs from the pan onto the paper towel to let the excess oil drain off. Season lightly with salt, if you like.

The crumbs will continue to crisp a bit as they cool. Store in an airtight container once they are fully cooled.

PARMIGIANO CROUTONS

Crunchy nuggets of bread enhanced with olive oil and Parmigiano are always welcome on a plate of salad or in a bowl of soup. The cheese will form a crisp frico-like coating on parts of the croutons, making them almost a snack on their own. Be forewarned.

MAKES ABOUT 2 CUPS (150 G)

Two 1-inch (2.5 cm) slices artisan-style bread (about 115 g total)

3 tablespoons extra-virgin olive oil

½ cup (50 g) finely grated Parmigiano-Reggiano cheese

Kosher salt and freshly ground black pepper

Preheat the oven to 400°F (200°C).

Cut or tear the bread into chunks about 1 inch (2.5 cm) square. Ragged is good—no need for precision here—but just remember that these need to be able to fit on top of a bowl of soup, so nothing too giant.

Put the bread in a large bowl, drizzle on the olive oil, sprinkle on the Parmigiano, and season everything with salt and pepper. Toss until the bread has absorbed all the oil and the cheese is nicely distributed.

Spread the croutons onto a sheet pan and bake until they are browned on the first side, about 7 minutes. Flip the croutons and continue baking until everything is nicely browned and crisp around the edges, another 5 to 8 minutes. You want them browned and crisp on the outside but retaining a bit of chewiness on the inside.

Drain the croutons on paper towels for a few minutes. Once cool, store in an airtight container and use within a couple of days.

Or Try This Idea

Omit the cheese and just make nicely seasoned croutons.

Sungold Cherry Tomato and Summer Corn Salad

Sungold tomatoes are a superstar variety that I'd like to see in everyone's yard—easy to grow, very productive, and so sweet and fruity. But if you're not a gardener, look for them at your local farmers' market or even at a good grocery store, as lots of small farms grow them. And of course, this salad will be delicious with any type of sweet cherry tomato.

For the fresh herbs in this salad, try a mix of cilantro, basil, and mint, or pick just one or two if three seems extravagant. You can sauté the scallions and chile up to a few hours ahead, but don't mix the other ingredients until close to serving time.

I think the cherry tomatoes with scallions and chile are a great platform for other summer ingredients, so see the ideas below for more options.

SERVES 2 OR 3

Extra-virgin olive oil

5 or 6 scallions, roots and top 2 inches (5 cm) of green trimmed off, then thinly sliced crosswise

1 fresh hot chile, such as jalapeño, seeded and finely chopped

Kosher salt

Kernels from 2 large ears corn

1 pint (340 g) cherry tomatoes, preferably Sungold or a mix of yellow and red, halved

Freshly ground black pepper

Aleppo pepper or chile flakes

1 lime, halved

Small handful of mixed herbs (cilantro, basil, mint, flat-leaf parsley, dill, and/or chervil), roughly chopped or torn

In a large skillet, heat about 2 tablespoons olive oil over medium heat. Add the scallions and chile, sprinkle with a pinch of salt, and sauté until soft and fragrant but not browned, about 3 minutes.

Increase the heat a bit and add the corn. Sauté the corn quickly, just to take the raw edge off but no longer, about 1 minute. (Note: If your corn isn't super fresh, cook it a bit longer to be sure it's tender.)

Scrape the scallion-corn mixture into a large salad bowl and let it cool for a few minutes, then add the tomatoes and season with a bit more salt, a few twists of black pepper, and Aleppo pepper. Toss.

Squeeze on about half the lime juice, toss again, and taste, then add more lime juice to your liking. You want the sweetness of the tomatoes and corn to be dominant but balanced by the tang of the lime juice.

Drizzle a few tablespoons of olive oil over the salad, toss again, and taste. Dial in the flavor with a bit more salt, Aleppo pepper, and/or lime juice, then add the fresh herbs and give the salad one final toss. Serve soon.

Or Try These Ideas

FETA AND TANGY PEPPERS: Add 4 ounces (115 g) feta cheese, cut into ½-inch (1.25 cm) cubes, and 3 tablespoons minced seeded peperoncini.

continues

MOZZARELLA AND RED PEPPER: Add 4 ounces (115 g) tiny balls of fresh mozzarella or large balls cut into ½-inch (1.25 cm) cubes and 1 seeded roasted red pepper cut into ½-inch (1.25 cm) squares. Use a nice red wine vinegar instead of lime juice.

WATERMELON AND MINT: Add about 1 cup diced watermelon (flick out most of the seeds if you can) and use mint as your herb.

TAHINI AND CUCUMBER: Omit the corn and add 1 large cucumber, peeled, seeded, and cut into ½-inch (1.25 cm) cubes. Instead of lime juice, dress the salad with a spoonful or two of tahini that's been thinned with lemon juice and seasoned with some grated garlic.

ROAST CHICKEN AND CROUTONS: Make it a main dish salad by adding about 6 ounces (175 g) shredded or diced roast chicken and a big handful of Parmigiano Croutons (page 79). Increase the lemon and olive oil and let the salad sit a few minutes so the croutons soak up some liquid.

Semi-Classic Panzanella

I call this "semi-" because I don't think Italians would include sautéed corn in a classic version. But panzanella is a brilliant way to feature all manner of delicious ingredients. As with any good platform, the foundational elements—the bread, tomatoes, vinegar, and olive oil—need to be excellent. The magic happens when those ingredients mingle, the tomatoes release juices, the bread drinks them up, and the proverbial whole becomes much more than the sum of its parts.

You want an artisan-type bread that has a light, airy texture, such as ciabatta or even focaccia. Choose tomatoes that are very ripe and juicy; even a shade overripe is fine. You'll need to let the salad sit for about 30 minutes, so plan accordingly.

SERVES 2 OR 3

About 8 ounces (225 g) airy bread, such as ciabatta, torn into 1- to 2-inch (2.5 to 5 cm) pieces

Extra-virgin olive oil

2 tablespoons (30 g) butter, melted

2 garlic cloves, grated or very finely chopped

Kosher salt and freshly ground black pepper

Kernels from 1 ear corn

2 large very ripe tomatoes, cored and cut into 1½-inch (4 cm) chunks

1 large or 2 small cucumbers, peeled, halved, seeded, and cut into ½-inch (1.25 cm) slices

2 tablespoons sherry vinegar or good red wine vinegar, plus more to taste

Chile flakes

1 roasted red pepper, peeled, cored, and cut into pieces

Small handful of basil, mint, or flat-leaf parsley leaves, torn or roughly chopped

Preheat the oven to 375°F (190°C).

Spread the bread on a sheet pan. In a small bowl, stir together 2 tablespoons olive oil, the melted butter, and grated garlic. Pour this over the bread, scooting the bread around so it's evenly coated. Season lightly with salt and pepper. Toast until just lightly golden and crisp around the edges but still soft inside, 10 to 12 minutes. Set aside to cool completely; don't eat all of it.

Meanwhile heat a glug of olive oil in a small skillet over medium-high heat, add the corn, season with salt and pepper, and cook just until the corn is tender; cool. In a large bowl, combine the tomatoes, cucumbers, and vinegar. Season generously with salt, black pepper, and a little pinch of chile flakes and toss. Let the vegetables macerate for 20 to 30 minutes; you want to encourage juices.

Add the cooled bread to the vegetables, toss, let sit for a few minutes, then toss again. You want the bread to be nicely moistened with the juices. Fold in the roasted pepper and corn, along with any optional add-ins.

Drizzle on about ¼ cup (60 ml) olive oil and toss again. Taste for seasoning, adding more salt, pepper, chile flakes, vinegar, and/or oil until you have a nice, slightly sloppy consistency and bright flavor. Finish by tossing with the fresh herbs.

Optional Add-Ins

- Small amount of very thinly sliced red onion, soaked in ice water for 20 minutes, drained, and blotted dry
- One 15-ounce (425 g) can chickpeas or white beans, rinsed and drained (or 1½ cups beans cooked from scratch, of course!)
- 1 or 2 cups shredded roast chicken
- 1 cup 1-inch (2.5 cm) pieces leftover grilled steak

WILL I KILL MY TOMATOES IF
I PUT THEM IN THE REFRIGERATOR?

A question of eternal debate among cooks is "Should I put my tomatoes in the refrigerator?" We're admonished by food writers like me (until now!) that time in the fridge will mute the flavors of a ripe tomato. Yet keeping ripe tomatoes on the counter, especially in summer for those of us without central air-conditioning, has its own problems such as fruit flies and hastening the demise of said ripe tomato as it sits for a few days in a warm kitchen.

I recently ventured down the rabbit hole of scientific studies on this topic, and though my dip into the pool of research was only in the shallow end, I discovered information that has changed my tomato-storing behavior and I hope will be of use to you.

First, let's take a quick look at what contributes to flavor in tomatoes. Much of a tomato's flavor comes from sugars, acids, and protein-related compounds (including the amino acid glutamate, which helps create proteins), but the substances that make tomatoes taste so beguilingly like tomatoes are called volatile compounds. You don't perceive these with your tongue, as you do the five basic flavors of sweet, salty, sour, bitter, and umami/savory; rather, you perceive volatile compounds with your most finely tuned sense organ, your nose.

Tomatoes contain hundreds of these aroma compounds, but scientists have isolated sixteen that seem to be what makes a tomato taste like a tomato.

These aroma compounds are activated by genes. When the temperature of a tomato goes below about 53°F (12°C), the genes shut off and no more compounds are produced; this effect is even greater when the temperatures drop into refrigerator range of 41°F (5°C) or below.

This gene shutdown is a disaster for flavor, because, unlike the sugars and acids in the tomato, which, once developed, can't really go anywhere—they stay in the tomato—volatile compounds need to be constantly replenished. They evaporate easily, and they "escape" through the stem scar of the tomato. So when the genes get cold and stop producing, there are no more volatile compounds and no more unique tomato flavor. A simplification, of course, but that's the idea.

But here's the happy revelation in all this: the genes don't stop making delicious aroma compounds until they've been in the cold *for around seven days*! One researcher tested tomatoes straight from the vine (Day 0), and again after one, three, and seven days. No reduction in the levels of aroma compounds was detected in the Day 1 or Day 3 samples, only in the Day 7 sample. (Note that the researchers checked to see whether the aroma compounds would return once the tomato was brought back to room temperature, but there was only a slight recovery after one day at 68°F/20°C.)

Did the aroma deterioration begin at four days? Does the flavor fall off a cliff or decline slowly? Who knows? But what I know is that a ripe tomato from the garden or farmers' market is "safe" in the fridge for up to three days, which to me is a very workable amount of time. I may not be ready to eat or cook with tomatoes the minute I bring them into my kitchen, but I certainly will get to them within three days.

Unfortunately, commercially produced tomatoes are pretty much guaranteed to have spent way more than seven days in the cold, whether riding in a distributor's truck from Florida, being stashed at a wholesaler's warehouse, or waiting in the walk-in at the grocery store. One more reason to avoid commercial tomatoes when possible.

Plums, Tomatoes, and Blueberries in Spiced Pomegranate Molasses Dressing

Fruit salad doesn't always have to be on the sweet side, and it certainly doesn't have to be boring. Here tomatoes are paired with sweet plums, which I think have a natural affinity with tomatoes, as well as with blueberries, for a contrast in shape. The fruit is dressed in a tangy vinaigrette with some punch from jalapeño. Have fun playing with the colors of your tomatoes and plums, both of which come in red, purple, magenta, gold, and green.

Pomegranate molasses, also called pomegranate syrup, is a condiment popular throughout the Middle East, and it's made from—you guessed it—pomegranate juice that's been cooked down into a syrup. Reminiscent of balsamic vinegar with its deep, sweet-tart flavor, pomegranate molasses is an excellent dressing for tomato salads in general. Look for brands that don't contain added sugar.

SERVES 3 OR 4

2 tablespoons pomegranate molasses

2 teaspoons balsamic vinegar or sherry vinegar

1 teaspoon sugar, plus more as needed

About 1 teaspoon finely chopped fresh hot chile, such as jalapeño

Kosher salt

Aleppo pepper or chile flakes

1 pound (450 g) tomatoes, cored and cut into chunks, or halved cherry tomatoes

½ pound (225 g) plums, pitted and cut into wedges

½ pint (150 g) blueberries

½ cup (15 g) roughly chopped fresh cilantro and mint (about half and half)

Extra-virgin olive oil

½ cup (60 g) chopped lightly toasted pistachios (optional)

In a medium bowl, whisk together the pomegranate molasses, vinegar, sugar, chile, ½ teaspoon salt, and a little pinch of Aleppo pepper. Let the dressing sit for 10 minutes. Taste and adjust the balance of the dressing with any of the ingredients; you want it to dance between sweet, tart, hot, and salty.

In a large bowl, combine the tomatoes, plums, and blueberries and pour on the dressing. Toss gently, taste, and adjust the seasoning once the fruit juices have had a chance to mingle with the dressing.

Add the herbs, drizzle with about 2 tablespoons olive oil, and toss again. Top with the pistachios, if using, and serve right away.

Or Try This Idea

Try this on whipped ricotta (from the Farro Salad, page 102). Substitute basil for the mint or the cilantro.

Tomato-Peach Salad
with Lime-Ginger Dressing

The starting point for this salad is nuoc cham, a Vietnamese dipping sauce and dressing made with fish sauce, lime juice, and chiles, lightly sweetened with sugar. Part of what I find compelling about the flavor of tomatoes is the umami, that hard-to-describe savory quality that lies underneath the sweet and tangy flavor of a ripe tomato. And fish sauce is like umami in a bottle, so it's a natural partner.

The salad is deceptive, as it's very easy to make and doesn't look super dramatic, but the flavors are mind-blowingly delicious. Of course, use the ripest peaches you can find so their sweetness contributes to the tension of the flavors.

SERVES 3 OR 4

1 tablespoon fish sauce, preferably Red Boat

1 tablespoon fresh lime juice

1 tablespoon minced fresh hot chile, such as jalapeño or serrano

2 teaspoons minced shallot or onion

1 teaspoon sugar

½ teaspoon grated or very finely chopped fresh ginger

2 medium tomatoes (about ½ pound/225 g total), cored and cut into wedges

2 medium peaches or nectarines (about ½ pound/ 225 g total), cut into wedges (peel the peaches only if the skin seems super fuzzy)

About ½ cup (15 g) lightly packed roughly chopped fresh herbs, such as cilantro, basil, and/or mint

In a small bowl, whisk together the fish sauce, lime juice, chile, shallot, sugar, and ginger. Let the dressing sit for at least 20 minutes, or up to 1 day (in the fridge if longer than 2 hours), to let the flavors develop.

Arrange the tomatoes and peaches on a platter or in a shallow bowl and drizzle the dressing all over. Top with the chopped herbs and serve right away.

Tomato, Peach, and Red Pepper Salad with Burrata

This salad can only be described as "voluptuous," with ripe tomatoes and juicy peaches cavorting with creamy pieces of burrata. Some burratas can be very runny, so wait until right before serving to rip into yours, lest too much creamy goodness escapes onto the platter. Once a true specialty product, burrata is showing up at many ordinary grocery stores in the specialty cheese section, but if you can't find it, use fresh mozzarella and rip rather than slice it.

SERVES 4

2 peaches or nectarines, cut into wedges (if the peaches are very fuzzy, peel them first)

2 large tomatoes, cored and cut into wedges

1 tablespoon sherry vinegar or balsamic vinegar

Kosher salt or flaky salt

1 ball burrata cheese (about 8 ounces/225 g) or fresh mozzarella

½ cup (125 g) roughly chopped drained oil-packed hot red peppers, such as Mama Lil's or Calabrian chiles (if the peppers are very spicy, you might want to reduce the amount)

Extra-virgin olive oil

About ½ cup (15 g) lightly packed sliced fresh basil leaves (or a mix of basil and mint)

Arrange the peach and tomato wedges on a platter or individual plates. Sprinkle on the vinegar and season with salt.

Pull apart the burrata and dollop it on top of or next to the peaches and tomatoes. Distribute the red peppers over the salad and give everything a nice drizzle of olive oil. Finish with a shower of the basil. Serve right away.

Watermelon, Cherry Tomato, and Cucumber Salad in Smoky Lime Vinaigrette

Ideal for the hottest days of summer, this salad is substantial enough to serve as supper on its own, but it's a winning accompaniment to anything from the grill. For me, that would be a tri-tip or a big fat rib eye, sliced and arranged on the same platter as the salad, so the juices commingle.

SERVES 4

1 pint cherry tomatoes, ideally Sungolds (or use larger tomatoes cut into chunks)

Kosher salt

About 2 cups 1-inch (2.5 cm) cubes watermelon, seeds flicked out as much as possible, chilled

1 English cucumber, peeled if the skin seems tough, cut into ½-inch (1.25 cm) slices (if you can find lemon cucumbers, use those and just cut into dice), chilled

Smoky Lime Vinaigrette (recipe follows)

7 to 8 ounces (200 to 225 g) feta, preferably Valbreso, a creamy French sheep's-milk cheese, cut into ½-inch (1.25 cm) cubes

½ cup (15 g) roughly chopped fresh cilantro, mint, or basil (or a mix)

Cut the cherry tomatoes in half and put them in a sieve set over a bowl to catch the juices. Toss with a pinch of salt and set aside while you prepare the rest of the salad ingredients.

Pile the tomatoes, watermelon, and cucumber into a large bowl. Pour any accumulated tomato juices into the vinaigrette, whisk to blend, taste, and do a final seasoning adjustment—you want the dressing to be lively and slightly sweet. Pour the dressing over the salad and toss gently to mix.

Add the feta and herbs and toss again very gently, trying not to crush the feta. Serve right away. Or if you want to make this ahead—to bring to a picnic, for example—add the dressing only right before serving; otherwise, the watermelon will lose its crunch.

SMOKY LIME VINAIGRETTE

MAKES ABOUT ½ CUP (120 ML)

2 tablespoons fresh lime juice

1 tablespoon sherry vinegar or white wine vinegar

1 teaspoon sweet or hot smoked paprika

1 teaspoon sugar

Kosher salt

⅓ cup (80 ml) extra-virgin olive oil

In a small bowl, whisk together the lime juice, vinegar, smoked paprika, sugar, and ¼ teaspoon salt until the sugar has dissolved. Gradually whisk in the oil until the dressing is creamy and blended. Taste and adjust the seasoning as necessary.

A Selection of Vinaigrettes for Tomatoes and More

A vinaigrette is a powerful component in a cook's repertoire. Quick to make, these bright dressings can turn juicy heirloom or colorful cherry tomatoes into a centerpiece salad or a topping for grilled vegetables, steak, or fish. Just remember that the tomato juices will dilute the dressings a bit, so be sure they are highly seasoned.

CAESAR-STYLE VINAIGRETTE

My go-to dressing, this umami-packed vinaigrette tastes good on pretty much everything. Toss chunks of tomato and croutons with a spoonful, and you've got a satisfying salad. Or top slices of grilled bread with some roasted tomatoes and a drizzle of the dressing for an easy crostini.

MAKES ABOUT ½ CUP (120 ML)

1 tablespoon plus 1 teaspoon finely grated Parmigiano-Reggiano cheese

1 teaspoon finely grated lemon zest

2 tablespoons fresh lemon juice, or more to taste

1 teaspoon Dijon mustard

2 or 3 oil-packed anchovy fillets

1 or 2 garlic cloves

Kosher salt and freshly ground black pepper

6 tablespoons (90 ml) extra-virgin olive oil

In a food processor, combine the cheese, lemon zest, lemon juice, mustard, anchovies, garlic, ½ teaspoon salt, and several twists of black pepper. Pulse several times until the ingredients are mostly blended, scraping down the sides of the bowl as needed. With the motor running, slowly pour in the oil and process until the vinaigrette is creamy and blended. Taste and adjust the flavor with more lemon, salt, and/or pepper.

Refrigerate the dressing in an airtight container for up to 2 days (I think the anchovy flavor oxidizes after longer than that).

TANGERINE–BROWN BUTTER VINAIGRETTE

This dressing has a few more steps than a regular whisk-in-one-bowl vinaigrette, but the results are worth it, with the brown butter creating a luscious texture and nutty flavor. Drizzle it onto sliced tomatoes, or fold with halved Sungold cherry tomatoes and use it to top a piece of fish hot from the grill.

MAKES ABOUT ½ CUP (120 ML)

2 tangerines

2 tablespoons sherry vinegar

1 tablespoon finely chopped shallot

4 tablespoons (60 g) butter

½ teaspoon Dijon mustard

1 tablespoon extra-virgin olive oil

Kosher salt

Aleppo pepper or chile flakes

1 tablespoon thinly sliced fresh chives (optional)

Finely grate about 1 teaspoon zest from one of the tangerines and set aside. Squeeze the juice from the tangerines and measure out ½ cup (120 ml). Watch out for seeds!

Put the tangerine zest, tangerine juice, vinegar, and shallot into a small saucepan and bring to a simmer over medium heat. Simmer, stirring often, until the liquid is reduced by about half, to ¼ cup (60 ml). Transfer to a small bowl and cool.

In another small saucepan, brown the butter following the instructions on page 155.

Whisk the mustard into the tangerine mixture, then whisk in the brown butter and olive oil. Season with a pinch each of salt and Aleppo pepper, then taste and adjust the seasoning. Stir in the chives, if using.

Use right away or refrigerate in an airtight container for up to 4 days. The butter will solidify in the cold, so take the vinaigrette out of the refrigerator at least 30 minutes before using it.

TOMATO-GINGER VINAIGRETTE

Two forms of tomato—sun-dried tomatoes and tomato paste—create layers of flavor, and when you use this dressing on fresh tomatoes, you've got a delicious triple threat. Try this on a caprese salad, or make a quick antipasto by rolling a strip of roasted red pepper around a dollop of ricotta or goat cheese and spooning on some dressing.

MAKES ABOUT ⅔ CUP (160 ML)

2 tablespoons apple cider vinegar

1 teaspoon finely grated orange zest

1 tablespoon fresh orange juice

1 tablespoon finely chopped oil-packed or other soft sun-dried tomato

1 teaspoon finely chopped fresh ginger

½ teaspoon Dijon mustard

½ teaspoon tomato paste

½ teaspoon sugar

Kosher salt and freshly ground black pepper

Few drops of hot sauce

6 tablespoons (90 ml) extra-virgin olive oil

In a small bowl, whisk the vinegar, orange zest, orange juice, sun-dried tomato, ginger, mustard, tomato paste, sugar, ½ teaspoon salt, several twists of black pepper, and hot sauce.

Gradually whisk in the olive oil until the dressing is emulsified and creamy. Taste and adjust the flavor balance until the dressing is sweet-tart-salty.

Refrigerate in an airtight container for up to 1 week. Whisk again just before using.

LEMON AND THYME VINAIGRETTE

Lemon thyme would be gorgeous in this dressing.

MAKES ABOUT ¾ CUP (180 ML)

1 tablespoon finely grated lemon zest

¼ cup (60 ml) fresh lemon juice

2 teaspoons chopped fresh thyme

2 garlic cloves, very finely chopped

½ teaspoon sugar

Kosher salt and freshly ground black pepper

⅛ teaspoon chile flakes or Aleppo pepper

½ cup (120 ml) extra-virgin olive oil

In a small bowl, whisk together the lemon zest, lemon juice, thyme, garlic, sugar, ½ teaspoon salt, several twists of black pepper, and the chile flakes until the sugar and salt have dissolved. Whisk in the olive oil. Taste and adjust the flavor with more of any of the ingredients. Refrigerate in an airtight container for up to 1 week.

Grilled Bread Salad with Tomatoes, Shrimp, Lemon, and Thyme

I love the kiss of smoke the grill brings to this main-dish, company-worthy salad, especially the way the scallions sweeten and soften on the grill. While you've got the fire going, grill a few lemon slices as well, though that's optional. Many recipes direct you to oil your tomatoes before grilling so they don't stick to the grates, but I say don't do it! The tomatoes will be tricky enough to wrangle on the grill without being slicked with oil.

SERVES 4

1 pound (450 g) large or jumbo shrimp, preferably wild, peeled and deveined

Lemon and Thyme Vinaigrette (page 95)

1 small cucumber, peeled, halved, seeded, and diced

1 tablespoon drained capers

½ cup (90 g) pitted Kalamata olives, halved

Three to four 1-inch (2.5 cm) slices ciabatta or other loose-textured artisan bread

Extra-virgin olive oil

1 bunch scallions (about 6), root ends trimmed

1 lemon, thinly sliced (optional)

Kosher salt

1 pint (340 g) cherry tomatoes

½ cup (15 g) lightly packed roughly chopped fresh cilantro or mint (or, ideally, a mix of the two)

Freshly ground black pepper

Aleppo pepper or chile flakes

NOTE

Don't dress the shrimp more than 30 minutes ahead of grilling them, or they'll get mushy from the lemon juice.

In a medium bowl, toss the shrimp with ¼ cup (60 ml) of the vinaigrette. Set aside. Put the remaining dressing in a bowl large enough to hold all the salad ingredients and add the cucumber, capers, and olives. Toss to mix.

Heat a grill to medium.

You should grill the bread first, but grill the other ingredients in the order that makes sense for the size of your grill surface, your fire, etc.

Grill the bread until nicely browned on both sides, about 3 minutes per side. Brush both sides of the bread with olive oil while the bread is still warm. When the bread is cool enough to handle, tear it into rough 1-inch (2.5 cm) pieces and toss about half of them into the salad bowl with the cucumbers. Reserve the other half (this way, some bread pieces will get soft and some will stay crunchy).

. Grill the scallions until quite browned and slightly collapsed, 10 to 15 minutes. Take your time with these so they become soft and sweet inside rather than just blackened on the outside. Cut into 1-inch (2.5 cm) pieces and toss into the salad bowl.

If using lemon slices, brush them with a bit of oil and season with salt. Grill over a section of the fire where they can slowly caramelize rather than blacken too quickly. Once they're nicely browned and the rinds are soft and chewy, cut into quarters or smaller pieces and set aside.

continues

Grill the shrimp until just opaque in the center, 4 to 8 minutes, depending on the size. Set aside.

Grill the tomatoes until the skins take on some color and they start to burst, but if they threaten to collapse so much that they'll fall through the grates or otherwise are in jeopardy, remove from the grill immediately. The goal is for the tomatoes to be lightly caramelized and very juicy. Add the tomatoes to the salad bowl.

Add the reserved bread, the grilled lemon (if using), and herbs to the salad bowl and give everything a thorough toss. Let sit for another 5 minutes so the dry bread soaks up a bit of the juices and then taste and adjust the seasoning with black pepper and Aleppo pepper and more salt and/or olive oil.

Divide among four wide bowls or plates, arrange one-quarter of the shrimp on each salad, drizzle another little thread of oil over the salads, and serve right away.

BLT Salad

Here you'll find all the flavors of the beloved sandwich, but with less bread and way more tomatoes. I use very crisp and dense romaine hearts because I adore the texture—a key element in any salad—but the salad will also be delicious with iceberg or a softer lettuce such as Bibb.

Plentiful bread crumbs stand in for the sandwich bread, and to emphasize the B in BLT, the crumbs are fried in bacon fat, but you could use olive oil, or if you have a batch of Shaggy Bread Crumbs (page 78) already made, go ahead and use them. I love the way crumbs integrate with the salad better than larger croutons could, meaning you'll get crisp crunch in every bite. This salad would be awesome with Classic Roasted Tomatoes (page 48) in place of fresh; depending on the size, two or three roasted halves per person would be a good amount.

SERVES 2 OR 3

1 pound (450 g) tomatoes, preferably a mix of colors and types

Kosher salt

4 to 6 slices bacon

Extra-virgin olive oil

1 large slice or 2 smaller slices rustic bread, such as ciabatta or sourdough, torn into large irregular crumbs

Freshly ground black pepper

1 small heart romaine lettuce, halved lengthwise and cut crosswise into sections, or 2 small Little Gem lettuces, cut into wedges

Creamy Salad Dressing (recipe follows)

Core the tomatoes and cut them into 1-inch (2.5 cm) chunks; or, if using cherry tomatoes, cut them in half. Season lightly with salt, pile the tomatoes into a colander or sieve set over a bowl (to catch the juices, which will be used to make the creamy salad dressing), and let drain while you prepare the rest of the salad.

Line a plate with paper towels to drain the bacon. In a skillet, cook the bacon over medium heat, taking the time to get all of the slices evenly crisp. Fatty bacon is delicious, but you don't want that chewy uncooked fat texture here. Drain on the paper towels.

Line another plate with more paper towels. Pour off all but 1 tablespoon of the bacon fat from the pan. Add 1 tablespoon olive oil and heat over medium-high heat. Drop one of the bread pieces into the fat—if it sizzles nicely, add the rest. If not, continue heating the fat and oil for a few more seconds. Add all the bread crumbs to the pan and shake the pan to coat them with fat and distribute them evenly across the bottom.

Cook the crumbs over medium heat until they are deep golden brown all over. Take your time with this; if you rush things, you may end up burning the crumbs. Transfer the crumbs to the paper towels to drain and season them lightly with salt and pepper. They will crisp as they cool.

Arrange the lettuce in a serving bowl or on plates and top with the tomatoes. Drizzle the lettuce and tomatoes with a generous amount of the dressing. Crumble the bacon over the tomatoes and then scatter the crumbs over everything. Serve right away, passing the remaining dressing at the table.

continues

CREAMY SALAD DRESSING

MAKES ABOUT ¼ CUP (60 ML)

3 tablespoons mayonnaise, preferably Hellmann's or Best Foods

2 tablespoons whole-milk yogurt (Greek or regular) or 1 tablespoon sour cream

2 teaspoons white wine vinegar or apple cider vinegar

Tomato juices reserved from BLT Salad (page 99)

Kosher salt and freshly ground black pepper

Tiny pinch of Aleppo pepper or cayenne pepper

Sugar, if needed

1 tablespoon finely chopped fresh flat-leaf parsley (optional)

In a small bowl, whisk together the mayonnaise, yogurt, and vinegar until smooth. Whisk in enough of the reserved tomato juices to thin the dressing to a nice pourable consistency. Season generously with salt, black pepper, and Aleppo pepper. Taste and adjust the seasoning, adding a pinch of sugar if needed to keep the dressing tangy but not sharp. Add the parsley, if using.

Farro Salad with Sungolds, Mint, Roasted Red Pepper, and Cucumber on Whipped Ricotta

A bed of cooked grains is a perfect platform for a tomato-focused salad, adding substance to make the salad more of a meal, all the while drinking up the sweet juices from the tomatoes and other vegetables. Here the grains are elevated with a swoosh of creamy whipped ricotta on the plate.

SERVES 4 TO 6

Whipped Ricotta

About 1 cup (250 g) whole-milk ricotta, preferably Calabro or Organic Valley

Extra-virgin olive oil

Kosher salt

Salad

2½ cups (390 g) cooked farro

2 tablespoons sherry vinegar or red wine vinegar, plus more to taste

Kosher salt

Chile flakes

1 pint (340 g) Sungold or other cherry tomatoes

1 medium cucumber

1 roasted red bell pepper, peeled, cored, seeded, and cut into ½-inch (1.25 cm) pieces

½ cup (15 g) roughly chopped fresh mint

Extra-virgin olive oil

MAKE THE WHIPPED RICOTTA: Put the ricotta in a food processor and pulse a few times to break it up. With the motor running, add about 2 tablespoons olive oil and ¼ teaspoon salt and process until creamy, stopping and scraping down the sides of the processor bowl if necessary. Taste and adjust with more salt and/or olive oil until it's delicious. Set aside.

ASSEMBLE THE SALAD: Put the farro in a large bowl, drizzle on the vinegar, season with a big pinch each of salt and chile flakes, and toss thoroughly.

Cut the tomatoes in half and add to a second bowl, along with any juices. Season with a pinch of salt.

Peel the cucumber, cut in half lengthwise, scrape out the seeds with a teaspoon, and cut into small pieces (if using Persian cucumbers, you can leave the seeds in and simply slice the cukes). Add to the tomatoes, along with the red pepper and half the mint. Let sit for about 5 minutes to get juicy.

Add the tomatoes and friends to the farro and toss well. Let sit for about 5 minutes, then taste and adjust the seasoning, keeping in mind that the whipped ricotta will add some salt. Add about 3 tablespoons olive oil and toss and taste again.

Spread a thick swoosh of ricotta on each individual plate or a serving platter. Pile the farro salad on top and finish with the remaining herbs.

Or Try This Idea

Instead of ricotta, use 7 or 8 ounces (200 or 225 g) feta, preferably a sheep's-milk feta that is sweet and creamy. You may need to add more olive oil in order to get a nice whipped consistency.

Upgraded Niçoise Salad with Roasted Tomatoes and Deviled Eggs

A Niçoise salad is an excellent example of a "composed salad," one in which the elements aren't tossed together but rather are presented as independent entities that work together on the plate. Because each component needs to stand alone, it's nice to elevate them—hard-boiled eggs get deviled, boiled potatoes get dressed in a mustard-caper dressing, and tomatoes get roasted to amp up their savory sweetness. A bit more work than the classic Niçoise, yes, but the "upgrades" make this version company-worthy for sure.

SERVES 4 AS A MAIN DISH

4 large hard-boiled eggs

1 tablespoon Dijon mustard, plus more to taste

2 tablespoons mayonnaise, plus more to taste

Kosher salt and freshly ground black pepper

½ pound (225 g) thin-skinned boiling potatoes, preferably new potatoes

2 tablespoons white wine vinegar

1 tablespoon drained capers, roughly chopped

Extra-virgin olive oil

½ pound (225 g) green beans, stem ends snapped or trimmed off

1 teaspoon finely grated lemon zest

8 anchovy fillets, rinsed and patted dry

1 pound (450 g) Classic Roasted Tomatoes (page 48) or Cherry Tomato Confit (page 231)

Two 5-ounce (142 g) cans good tuna in olive oil, drained and broken into a few chunks

continues

Peel the eggs, halve them lengthwise, and pop the yolks into a small bowl. Add 1 teaspoon of the mustard, the mayonnaise, and a generous pinch each of salt and pepper. Mash the yolks and other ingredients with a fork until you have a nice texture. Taste and adjust with more of any of the seasonings. Spoon the creamy yolk filling back into the whites and set aside, in the fridge if you're making the deviled eggs more than about 1 hour ahead of time.

If the potato skins are anything but thin and delicate, peel the potatoes, or at least peel off the tough-looking parts. If the potatoes are larger than a lime, cut them in half. Put the potatoes in a large saucepan, cover with water by about 3 inches (7.5 cm), season the water with about 1 tablespoon kosher salt, and bring to a boil. Boil the potatoes until they are completely tender, about 20 minutes.

Scoop out ½ cup (120 ml) of the boiling water, then drain the potatoes. Put the potatoes back in the pan and let cool just until you can handle them; they should still be very warm. Cut them into large bite-size chunks. In a small bowl, stir the remaining 2 teaspoons mustard into the vinegar, pour over the warm potatoes, and toss gently until the dressing has been mostly absorbed by the potatoes. Add a few spoonfuls of the reserved cooking water to make the potatoes almost creamy. Add the capers and season generously with salt and black pepper. Taste and adjust the seasoning. Drizzle with about ¼ cup (60 ml) olive oil, toss again, and set aside.

Put the green beans in a small skillet or shallow saucepan, add enough water to just barely cover them, then add about 1 teaspoon salt, cover, and bring to a boil. Adjust the heat to a strong simmer and simmer until the beans are very tender, 5 to 7 minutes, or longer depending on the age and size of your beans. If you like crisp-tender, that's fine, but I prefer

½ cup (120 g) pitted olives such as Niçoise, Lucques, picholine, Castelvetrano, or Kalamata

½ cup (15 g) lightly packed roughly chopped fresh basil and/or flat-leaf parsley

Nice bread, for serving

my green beans very tender. Drain, toss with a few drops of olive oil and the lemon zest, and season with salt and pepper. Taste and adjust the seasoning. Set aside.

To assemble the salad, arrange the potato salad in the center of a grand platter or on individual plates, and perch the anchovy fillets casually on top. Then nestle the other elements—green beans, roasted tomato halves, deviled egg halves, a tumble of tuna—around the potatoes. Scatter the olives everywhere and shower the whole thing with the herbs. Serve right away, with some good bread on the side.

Caprese Salad, Reconsidered

A caprese salad—tomato, mozzarella, and basil—is a perfect dish, but that doesn't mean you have to eat it in exactly the same "format" every time. Jeans are perfect, too, but I'll wager you have more styles than just Levi's 501s in your wardrobe.

The classic caprese is slices of tomato, fresh mozzarella, and fresh basil leaves shingled on each other in a pretty pattern, drizzled with a bit of olive oil and sprinkled with salt. Always delicious, but if you want a new look, here are some riffs.

ROASTED CAPRESE: Use Classic Roasted Tomatoes (page 48) or Low and Slow Roasted Plum Tomatoes (page 164) instead of fresh tomatoes. This is a good strategy to use when your fresh tomatoes aren't quite ripe or flavorful.

CHUNKS, NOT SLICES: Use halved cherry tomatoes or chunks of large tomatoes, diced fresh mozzarella (or those tiny mozz balls called *ciliegine*), and fine shreds of fresh basil. Drizzle with olive oil, season with kosher salt and freshly ground black pepper, and toss gently. This format makes it easier for the tomato juices to coat the cheese and for the basil to perfume every bite.

PESTO, NOT WHOLE LEAVES: Whole herb leaves can be annoying to eat, so make a loose herb paste by whizzing a big handful of fresh basil leaves (add other tender herbs as well—mint, parsley, and cilantro would be yummy) with salt and olive oil in the food processor. Drizzle the sliced tomato and mozzarella with the pesto right before serving.

PLAY WITH TEMPERATURES: Instead of using fresh tomatoes, top a plate of sliced mozzarella with still-warm Blasted Cherry Tomatoes (page 151), spooning the pan juices over everything and topping it with some fine shreds of fresh basil.

PLAY WITH TEXTURES: Use burrata, that tender mozzarella ball with the creamy, flowing center, instead of regular fresh mozzarella. You can't really slice burrata, so just gently pull it into pieces, but be ready with the serving plate, because it's deliciously sloppy.

PLAY WITH TEMPERATURES AND TEXTURES: Spoon still-warm Blasted Cherry Tomatoes (page 151) over torn chunks of burrata.

ADD ANOTHER ELEMENT: Instead of just tomato, mozz, tomato, mozz, try tomato, mozz, roasted red pepper. Or even spoon on some spicy red peppers in oil, such as Calabrian peppers or Mama Lil's brand.

Greek Salad, Revisited

The elements of a classic Greek salad—chunks of ripe tomato, crisp cucumber, creamy-tangy feta, and briny black olives—work so perfectly together that it seems like there's little room for improvement. But if you want to get a taste of feta in every bite, rather than a sprinkling or a crumble, trying whipping the feta so you can scoop up a bit with each forkful.

SERVES 4

7 ounces (200 g) feta, preferably Valbreso, a creamy French sheep's-milk cheese

1 teaspoon grated lemon zest

Kosher salt and freshly ground black pepper

Aleppo pepper

Extra-virgin olive oil

1 tablespoon red wine vinegar

¼ teaspoon Dijon mustard

1 garlic clove, finely chopped

½ teaspoon dried oregano or dried mint

2 large or a few smaller tomatoes, cored and halved

1 large or 2 small cucumbers, peeled, halved lengthwise, seeded, and cut into slices ½ inch (1.25 cm) thick

Thin slices red onion, soaked in ice water, drained

Small handful of Kalamata or other good black olives

2 tablespoons drained capers

3 or 4 peperoncini, cored, seeded, and sliced (optional)

Several leaves fresh mint, torn or roughly chopped, 2 tablespoons chopped fresh dill, or both (optional)

In a food processor, combine the feta and lemon zest and season with salt, a few twists of black pepper, and a pinch of Aleppo pepper. Process until the cheese forms a rough puree. With the processor running, pour in 2 to 3 tablespoons olive oil (the amount will depend on how dry your feta is), scraping down the sides of the processor bowl as needed. Add a little more oil as needed to create a thick, creamy spread. Taste and adjust the seasoning with more salt, Aleppo pepper, and/or black pepper. Set aside.

In a large bowl, whisk together the vinegar, mustard, garlic, oregano, ¼ teaspoon salt, and several twists of black pepper. Whisk in about ¼ cup (60 ml) olive oil. Taste and adjust the seasoning as necessary to make an assertive dressing.

No more than about 15 minutes before serving, seed the tomatoes by giving the halves a gentle squeeze and then cut them into chunks. Add the tomatoes, cucumber, red onion, olives, capers, and peperoncini (if using) to the bowl with the dressing. (If you add the vegetables too soon, they will give off a lot of liquid and make things soggy.) Toss to coat everything well and let sit for about 5 minutes. Toss again, then taste and adjust the seasoning. If the flavor is a bit sharp, add more olive oil, but remember that the cheese will temper the vinegar's edge.

When you're ready to serve, spread a thick layer of the whipped feta on salad plates or a platter and pile the tomato mixture on top. Top with the fresh mint, if using.

Or Try This Idea

Spread the feta on lightly grilled bread and tumble the tomato mixture onto that, or add a big handful of Parmigiano Croutons (page 79) or Shaggy Bread Crumbs (78) to the tomato mixture a few minutes before serving, allowing the bread to soak up some of the juices.

French Lentils with Cherry Tomatoes, Wrinkly Green Beans, and Smoky Almonds

Firm, nutty French green lentils are great at soaking up vinaigrette; I actually prefer them in a salad rather than in a warm dish.

Re your green beans: no crisp-tender here; you want the green beans wrinkly and sweet, echoing the deep savoriness of the tomatoes and lentils. A vinaigrette studded with sun-dried tomatoes provides an acidic zing that brings the dish together.

SERVES 4

12 ounces (340 g) green beans, stem ends trimmed or snapped, halved if long enough to be unwieldy

Extra-virgin olive oil

Kosher salt and freshly ground black pepper

1 cup (200 g) French lentils

1 bay leaf

2 cups (480 ml) homemade or low-sodium canned chicken broth or water

2 tablespoons sherry vinegar or good red wine vinegar, plus more to taste

1 teaspoon finely chopped fresh thyme

1 teaspoon Dijon mustard

⅓ cup (50 g) finely chopped drained oil-packed sun-dried tomatoes

1 cup (180 g) cherry tomatoes, halved

¼ cup (7 g) roughly chopped fresh flat-leaf parsley

½ cup (70 g) roughly chopped smokehouse-style almonds or salted roasted almonds

Preheat the oven to 425°F (220°C).

Spread the green beans on a sheet pan, drizzle generously with olive oil, season with salt and pepper, and toss everything around to make sure all the beans are evenly coated.

Roast the green beans until they are very tender, fairly shriveled, and very sweet, 15 to 25 minutes, depending on the size and toughness of the beans. Let cool.

Meanwhile, combine the lentils, bay leaf, and chicken broth in a saucepan. The lentils should be covered by about 1 inch (2.5 cm), but if not, add water to that depth. Add 1 teaspoon salt, bring to a simmer, cover, and adjust the heat so the lentils simmer gently. Cook until they are fully tender but not falling apart, 15 to 25 minutes. Watch the liquid level—if the lentils have absorbed all the water before they're fully cooked, add a bit more water. If they are cooked and there's still liquid in the pan, drain the lentils in a sieve. Keep the lentils warm.

In a small bowl, whisk together the vinegar, thyme, and mustard. Add ¼ teaspoon salt and a few twists of black pepper, then whisk in ¼ cup (60 ml) olive oil. Stir in the sun-dried tomatoes. Taste and adjust the seasoning so the dressing is nice and zesty.

Put the still-warm lentils in a large bowl, add the vinaigrette, and toss gently. Let stand for about 10 minutes, toss again, and adjust the seasoning with more olive oil, vinegar, salt, and/or pepper. Gently fold in the tomatoes and green beans. Pile onto a serving platter and top with the parsley and chopped almonds.

Tomato Soups

Gazpacho #1—Blended and Smoky

This has to be the most refreshing soup on the planet, and a restorative one as well. It's literally a liquid salad, full of good-for-you vegetables, with a small amount of bread to create a creamy texture (you can skip the bread, but the soup won't have the same body). The flavors are quite intense, but they relax into balance as the ice melts. You could, of course, skip the ice and thin the soup with about ½ cup (120 ml) cold water, but I like this soup to be as cold as possible, which is why I use ice.

SERVES 4 AS A STARTER, 2 AS A MAIN COURSE

1½ pounds (680 g) tomatoes, cored and cut into chunks

About ½ pound (225 g) cucumber, peeled, halved lengthwise, seeded, and cut into chunks

1 roasted red bell pepper, peeled, cored, and seeded (from a jar is fine)

4 ounces (115 g) onion (about ½ small onion), cut into chunks

1 or 2 garlic cloves, smashed and peeled

1-ounce (30 g) slice of bread, preferably a nice artisan type, ripped into pieces

2 tablespoons sherry vinegar or good red wine vinegar

1 tablespoon sweet or hot smoked paprika (using hot paprika will make this soup quite spicy)

Kosher salt and freshly ground black pepper

¼ teaspoon Aleppo pepper

¼ cup (60 ml) extra-virgin olive oil, plus more for serving

¼ cup (7 g) lightly packed roughly chopped fresh cilantro, mint, flat-leaf parsley, and/or basil

4 small ice cubes

In a large bowl, combine the tomatoes, cucumber, roasted pepper, onion, garlic, bread, vinegar, smoked paprika, 2 teaspoons salt, several twists of black pepper, and the Aleppo pepper and toss thoroughly. Let macerate in the refrigerator for at least 1 hour, and up to overnight.

After the soup has macerated, add the olive oil and herbs and blend everything in a blender until completely smooth. Strain through a fine-mesh sieve into a bowl (or don't worry about the texture being perfect and skip the straining).

Divide the soup among shallow soup bowls. Put an ice cube in the center of each, top with your garnishes, and drizzle each bowl generously with more olive oil. Serve right away. Have your guests stir the ice into the soup as it melts.

Garnish options

Chopped cucumber, chopped red onion, Quick-Pickled Cherry Tomatoes (page 40), Shaggy Bread Crumbs (page 78), Parmigiano Croutons (page 79), crumbled feta, fried herbs, or tomato leaves

Gazpacho #2— Finely Chopped and Fresh

The success of this soup depends on your willingness to cut all the vegetables into very tiny dice. Get out the knife sharpener! The final texture is hard to describe, but if your tomatoes are nicely juicy and your chopping chops are on point, the result is a pleasing not-quite-liquid-but-not-a-salad consistency. The tomatoes, of course, need to be ripe and flavorful, and you'll want to set up your workstation so you can capture their juices as you chop; they are key to the "soupiness" of the soup.

The payoff for your diligence at the cutting board is a jewel-toned soup with an intriguing texture and all the bright flavors of summer in a bowl.

SERVES 2

2 tablespoons very finely chopped onion

2 tablespoons very finely chopped fresh hot chile, such as jalapeño

½ to 1 teaspoon very finely chopped garlic

1 tablespoon sherry vinegar or red wine vinegar

Kosher salt

1 pound (450 g) ripe, juicy tomatoes (don't use plum tomatoes)

1 tablespoon very finely chopped celery

1 cup (130 g) very finely chopped seeded peeled cucumber

½ cup (75 g) very finely chopped red bell or other sweet red pepper (try to peel off most of the skin using a vegetable peeler before chopping)

Extra-virgin olive oil

Freshly ground black pepper

Big pinch of chopped fresh herbs, such as flat-leaf parsley, dill, chervil, basil, cilantro, or mint

In a large bowl, combine the onion, chile, garlic, vinegar, and ½ teaspoon salt and let macerate while you prepare the other ingredients. This step tempers the harshness of the raw onion, chile, and garlic.

Set a fine-mesh sieve over the bowl of onion-chile mixture. Core the tomatoes, halve them through the equator, and squeeze the seeds into the sieve. Press on the seeds and gel to push the juices through the sieve into the bowl. Discard the seeds and replace the sieve over the bowl.

Cut the tomatoes into very thin slices, then cut across the slices to create tiny dice, ¼ inch (6 mm) or smaller, adding them to the sieve as you work. Try also to capture the juices as you work, tilting the cutting board to pour the juices into the sieve. Let the tomatoes sit in the sieve to drain as you finish prepping the other ingredients.

Add the diced tomatoes, celery, cucumber, bell pepper, and about 2 tablespoons olive oil to the bowl and toss to mix. Refrigerate until very cold. Taste and season generously with salt and black pepper.

Divide the gazpacho between two small soup bowls, drizzle with more olive oil, top with the chopped herbs, and serve immediately.

Gazpacho #3—
Clear and Intensely Tomatoey

I've been chasing this soup ever since I tasted the original inspiration many years ago in a tiny café in Faro, a town in the Algarve region of Portugal. My friend and I had been seeking good local food, but all we were finding was generic pizza and ham sandwiches until the desk clerk at our hotel told us about a place around the corner. Formica tables, football (soccer) game on the TV, very promising.

I ordered the soup, which came in a large stoneware bowl. I was puzzled because it looked like a bowl of water with a few chunks of onion, cucumber, and tomato in it. But that first spoonful of "water" blew my mind—such an intense tomato flavor, like a cold tomato consommé, bright and sharp with vinegar, which was quickly soothed with the glistening droplets of fragrant olive oil on the surface. I've never had anything like it in a restaurant since then and never could figure out how to make it at home until I started exploring tomato water, that magical elixir of fruit and umami.

I'm not giving precise measurements here, because it sort of depends on how much tomato water you have; the amount of vegetable chunks is up to you as well. (Pictured on page 112)

SERVES 1

A few slices red onion

About 1 teaspoon sherry vinegar or red wine vinegar

A big pinch of kosher salt

Small chunks of tomato

Small chunks of cucumber

Tomato Water (page 70), well chilled

Finishing-quality extra-virgin olive oil (see page 15)

A few leaves fresh oregano, marjoram, or summer savory, torn into small pieces

1 small ice cube (optional)

In a small bowl, combine the onion, vinegar, and salt. Soak the onion for 20 minutes.

In a cold soup bowl, combine the tomato, cucumber, and onion-vinegar mixture. Pour on tomato water to cover by 1 inch (2.5 cm) or so, taste and adjust with more salt if needed. Drizzle with olive oil, and scatter the herbs over the surface. Serve right away, very cold; if your ingredients aren't super cold, add an ice cube to the bowl.

Chilled Roasted Tomato, Corn, and Potato Soup

This rich but refreshing soup is inspired by classic vichyssoise, the French chilled potato and leek soup that's a good excuse to use a lot of cream. The richness is offset by mellow roasted tomatoes, with fresh corn contributing more sweetness. Make sure to allow enough time for chilling (at least four hours).

SERVES 4 TO 6

Extra-virgin olive oil

1 garlic clove, smashed and peeled

½ cup (75 g) finely chopped onion, preferably a sweet variety such as Vidalia or Walla Walla

Kosher salt

Pinch of Aleppo pepper or chile flakes

12 ounces (340 g) Yukon Gold potatoes, peeled and cut into small chunks

1 quart (1 L) homemade or low-sodium canned chicken broth or water

Kernels from 3 ears corn

1 recipe Classic Roasted Tomatoes (page 48); about 1 pound (450 g)

1½ cups (360 ml) heavy cream

¼ cup roughly chopped fresh dill or chives, or both

In a large saucepan or Dutch oven, heat a glug of olive oil over medium heat. Add the garlic and cook until it's very soft, fragrant, and light golden brown, about 3 minutes, breaking up the smashed clove a bit with your spatula.

Add the onion and a big pinch each of salt and Aleppo pepper and cook gently until the onion is very soft and sweet but not browned, about 8 minutes.

Add the potatoes, broth, and 2 teaspoons salt, bring to a simmer, and cook, partially covered, until the potatoes are just tender, about 20 minutes. Add the corn and continue simmering until the corn is very tender, 3 to 10 minutes, depending on the corn.

Transfer the soup to a blender, add the roasted tomatoes, and blend until very smooth. (Do this in batches if necessary.) Return the soup to the pan, straining it through a fine-mesh sieve if you want an ultra-smooth texture. Add the cream and simmer for about 5 minutes to cook off the raw cream flavor.

Taste the soup and season with more salt and/or Aleppo pepper. Chill thoroughly.

To serve, taste and adjust the seasoning again, ladle into serving bowls, and garnish with the herbs and a few droplets of olive oil.

Soup of the Season

You can use whatever seasonal produce looks good in your garden or at the market to make this soup, though the two constants are the corn (and resulting corn broth) and, of course, the tomatoes, which are a perfect bright contrast to the creamy flavor of the corn.

SERVES 4

4 ears corn, husked

1 quart (1 L) homemade or low-sodium canned chicken broth (or use all water or vegetable broth to make this vegetarian), plus more as needed

Kosher salt

Extra-virgin olive oil or butter

2 small zucchini or other summer squash (½ pound/ 225 g total), cut into ½-inch (1.25 cm) cubes

½ cup (75 g) chopped onion

¼ cup (30 g) chopped scallions, white and light green parts

½ cup (65 g) chopped celery

1 garlic clove, finely chopped

Freshly ground black pepper

½ pound (225 g) potatoes, such as Yukon Gold or a red-skinned variety (ideally a fresh potato from the season), peeled and cut into ½-inch (1.25 cm) cubes

½ pound (225 g) tomatoes, cut into small chunks

About ⅓ cup (10 g) lightly packed finely sliced fresh basil leaves

Cut the kernels off the corncobs and set the kernels aside. Put the corncobs in a large pot with the chicken broth, 1 quart (1 L) water, and 1 teaspoon salt. (Cut the corncobs in half if that allows them to fit better in the pot and be submerged by the liquid.) Bring to a gentle simmer and cook, partially covered, until the broth is sweet and corny and the liquid has reduced by about 25 percent (to about 6 cups/1.5 L), about 45 minutes. This will concentrate the flavors.

While the broth simmers, heat a glug of olive oil or a knob of butter in a medium skillet over medium-high heat. Add the zucchini and a pinch of salt. Let the zucchini sit undisturbed for about 1 minute to get a nice browned surface. Flip the zucchini over and brown more of the other surfaces. (You don't need to turn every single piece of zucchini; just shake the pan a bit and do your best.) Cook until the zucchini is browned and slightly tender but not at all mushy (it will continue to cook in the soup), another minute or so. Set aside.

In a large soup pot or Dutch oven, heat a small amount of olive oil over medium heat. Add the onion, scallions, celery, and garlic. Season lightly with salt and a few twists of black pepper. Cook gently until the vegetables are very sweet, fragrant, and translucent but not at all browned, about 4 minutes. If the corn broth is ready, proceed with the next step; if not, just set the pot off the heat.

When the corn broth is ready, strain it and see if you have 6 cups (1.5 L). If you don't quite have 6 cups (1.5 L), add water or chicken broth to complete the measurement. Add the strained corn broth to the soup pot, along with the potatoes and 2 teaspoons salt. Bring to a simmer and cook until the potatoes are tender, 15 to 20 minutes (pay attention, because small dice of new potatoes can cook quickly).

Add the tomatoes, sautéed zucchini, and reserved corn kernels and simmer just until everything is warmed through—you want the tomatoes to taste very fresh. Taste and adjust with more salt and/or pepper.

To serve, put a big pinch of the sliced basil in each soup bowl and ladle the hot soup on top.

Classic Tomato Soup, with Three Variations

I grew up loving Campbell's tomato soup—with Ritz crackers, of course—but I'm pretty sure that if I tasted it now, it wouldn't live up to the memories, so these days I make my own. This from-scratch tomato soup freezes brilliantly, so you can have all the convenience of canned soup but with much better flavor.

The basic soup is savory and satisfying, but it's also an excellent opportunity for variation. I'm including the versions I make most frequently, but you should feel free to ad-lib using your own favorite combinations. If you think you'll want to try a few versions, make a double or triple batch of this classic recipe; allow a little more cooking time at each of the stages, since your pot will be fuller. Note that the ginger doesn't make the soup taste gingery, per se; it just adds a note of complexity.

MAKES 6 CUPS (1.5 L)

One 28-ounce (794 g) can whole peeled tomatoes

Extra-virgin olive oil

1 cup (150 g) chopped onion

½ cup (65 g) finely chopped carrot

⅛ teaspoon chile flakes, plus more to taste

Kosher salt

1 or 2 garlic cloves, finely chopped

1 teaspoon finely chopped fresh ginger

1½ teaspoons sugar, or more to taste

1 quart (1 L) homemade or low-sodium canned chicken broth (or vegetable broth or water)

1 sprig fresh thyme

½ cup (15 g) roughly chopped fresh flat-leaf parsley or basil

Freshly ground black pepper

Break up the canned tomatoes by slashing them with a knife or snipping them with clean kitchen scissors while they're still in the can. (Alternatively, dump them into a bowl and squish them with your hands or a potato masher—watch out, as the juices will squirt out if you don't pierce the tomato with your fingers before you squeeze.) Set aside.

In a large soup pot or Dutch oven, heat a glug of oil over medium heat. Add the onion, carrot, chile flakes, and a pinch of salt. Cook until the vegetables are very soft, sweet, and fragrant but not at all browned, 8 to 10 minutes.

Add the garlic, ginger, sugar, and a bit more oil if the pan seems dry, and cook for another minute or two so the garlic and ginger soften.

Add the tomatoes, broth, thyme sprig, chopped herbs, and several twists of black pepper. Bring to a simmer and cook gently, uncovered, until the soup has reduced by about 25 percent and tastes rich and tomatoey, about 45 minutes.

Taste and adjust the seasoning with more salt, pepper, chile flakes, and/or sugar. Remove the thyme sprig; most of the leaves will have dispersed into the soup, so you just want to get the wiry stem out.

Now decide on your final texture: you can leave the soup chunky as is, blend about half so it's semi-chunky, or blend until smooth, straining out the seeds and other bits.

Serve hot, perhaps with a drizzle of olive oil . . . and a Ritz cracker or two.

continues

Or Try These Ideas

WHITE BEAN, ITALIAN SAUSAGE, PARMIGIANO:
Make the tomato soup as directed. Meanwhile, in a skillet, brown about 5 ounces (150 g) sweet or hot Italian sausage links until just cooked through. When the sausage is cool enough to handle, cut it into ½-inch (1.25 cm) slices and add to the soup. Add one 15-ounce (425 g) can cannellini or gigante beans, rinsed and drained (or 1½ cups white beans cooked from scratch), ½ cup (50 g) finely grated Parmigiano-Reggiano, and ¼ cup (7 g) sliced fresh basil leaves. Simmer everything gently for a few minutes to heat the additions and let the flavors marry. Taste, adjust the seasoning, and serve, with more Parmigiano to pass at the table.

MEDITERRANEAN FLAVORS: If possible, make this variation a day ahead and reheat it, as the flavors develop nicely with a bit of time. Make the tomato soup as directed; add half the soup to a blender and blend with 1 roasted red pepper, peeled and seeded—you can use jarred, if you like; piquillo peppers from Spain are nice—along with 1 teaspoon grated orange zest, ½ cup (120 ml) fresh orange juice, 1 tablespoon sweet or hot smoked paprika (hot paprika will make the soup quite spicy), and a small pinch of saffron threads. Pour the puree back into the remaining soup and simmer for a few minutes to let the saffron bloom and the other flavors blend. Taste and adjust the seasoning.

CREAM OF TOMATO SOUP WITH PARMIGIANO CROUTONS: Make the tomato soup as directed. Add about ¾ cup (180 ml) crème fraîche or heavy cream (I prefer the tanginess of crème fraîche) and simmer for about 5 minutes to cook off the raw cream flavor. Puree the soup and strain through a fine-mesh sieve back into the pot. Serve hot with Parmigiano Croutons (page 79).

TOMATOES FREEZE BEAUTIFULLY

If you're lucky enough to have the problem of too many tomatoes, your freezer is one quick and efficient solution. Tomatoes freeze well, lasting in good shape for 6 months or more when stored in an airtight bag or container in a freezer that's set for 0°F (−18°C) or colder.

The texture will change, however, so frozen tomatoes aren't appropriate for a salad or other dish in which you would use a raw fresh tomato. Think of thawed tomatoes from your freezer as more like canned tomatoes, perfect for sauces, soups, salsas, or pasta dishes.

Cherry tomatoes are the easiest to freeze. Simply remove any stems or leaves, rinse, shake off the water, and spread onto a baking sheet. Freeze uncovered until solid, then pile them into a freezer bag. Because they were frozen before you put them into the bag, they'll remain loose and separate, making it easy to take out only as many as you need.

Larger tomatoes should be processed in the same way, though it's best to cut out the stem area and cut larger tomatoes into halves or quarters. Freeze uncovered on a baking sheet until solid, then store in an airtight freezer bag or container. If you have a vacuum food saver, arrange the tomatoes unfrozen in a single layer in a large vacuum bag, seal, and then freeze.

You can peel your tomatoes before freezing, if you like, or freeze them with the skins and remove them once thawed. The freezing will loosen the skins in the same way as a dunking into boiling water does, making it easy to pluck the skins off as the tomatoes thaw.

You can also skip the thawing step and add frozen tomatoes directly to your pot. I often make dishes such as Flash-Sautéed Cherry Tomatoes, Lemon, and Tuna on Angel Hair Pasta (page 147) with frozen cherry tomatoes, allowing several extra minutes for the tomatoes to thaw in the pan.

Seafood and Tomato Soup with Smoky, Garlicky Grilled Bread

This dish is good any night of the week, but it also makes a fabulous dinner party main dish—you can prepare much of it ahead, and there's something festive about a big pot of cheery tomato soup fragrant with saffron and brimming with seafood. You can make it as modest or fancy as you like, using less expensive cod or rockfish or more lavish halibut. For the basic level, try just a white fish and shrimp, but to make it extra special, you can add mussels, clams, scallops . . . heck, throw in some lobster! If you can use homemade fish or shellfish stock, please do, but a mix of bottled clam juice and chicken or vegetable broth is just fine, as the dominant flavor of this dish will be tomato—as it should be.

SERVES 4

Grilled Bread

¼ cup (60 ml) extra-virgin olive oil

2 teaspoons sweet or hot smoked paprika

½ teaspoon ground cumin

Four ¾-inch (2 cm) slices of bread from a boule-style (round) or other fat loaf (or 8 slices if using a slender loaf like a baguette)

2 garlic cloves, halved lengthwise

Kosher salt

Soup

Extra-virgin olive oil

1 small fresh hot chile, such as jalapeño, seeded and very finely chopped

1½ tablespoons chopped garlic

Two 28-ounce (794 g) cans whole peeled tomatoes, drained and roughly chopped

1 cup (240 ml) dry white wine

3 cups (720 ml) fish stock (or a mixture of clam juice and homemade or low-sodium canned chicken broth; don't use all clam juice, because it would be too strong)

A large pinch of saffron threads

Kosher salt

1 pound (450 g) boneless halibut, cod, or other firm white fish, cut into 1-inch (2.5 cm) chunks

½ pound (225 g) shrimp, preferably wild, peeled and deveined (use any size, but if they are quite large, split them in half lengthwise so that there are more pieces in each portion)

1 pound (450 g) mussels, well scrubbed and debearded

1 pound (450 g) small clams, well scrubbed

Hot sauce

¼ cup (7 g) chopped fresh flat-leaf parsley, cilantro, or basil (or a mix)

GRILL THE BREAD: Heat a grill to medium (or heat the broiler or grill pan, if you're cooking indoors). In a small bowl, stir together the olive oil, smoked paprika, and cumin and keep nearby. Grill the bread until browned around the edges and lightly toasted all over, about 2 minutes per side. Brush both sides of the still-warm bread slices with the spiced oil mixture. When the bread is cool enough to handle, rub one side of each slice with the cut garlic. Season lightly with salt. Set aside.

MAKE THE SOUP: In a very large soup pot or Dutch oven (and I mean very large; mussels and clams take up a lot of room as they open), heat a generous glug of olive oil over medium heat. Add the chile and cook until softened, about 1 minute. Add the chopped garlic and cook until fragrant, another 30 seconds or so. Add the tomatoes and wine, increase the heat to medium-high, and simmer vigorously until the tomatoes are broken down and the mixture is slightly soupy, about 15 minutes.

Stir in the fish stock and saffron. Taste and then season lightly with salt (go easy if using clam juice, as it will be salty) and simmer to slightly reduce the broth and concentrate the flavors, about 5 minutes. Add the fish, shrimp, mussels, and clams (and any other seafood you're using, unless it's already cooked) and simmer until the fish and shrimp are opaque throughout and the shellfish have opened, 3 to 5 minutes more. Season to taste with more salt and some hot sauce.

Put 1 large or 2 small slices of the grilled bread in each of four wide soup bowls, ladle the soup on top, and sprinkle with the parsley. Serve right away, with a knife and fork as well as a spoon, and a big bowl for everyone's discarded shells.

Tomato Soup with Coconut, Chicken, and Chile

This soup is made with two batches of Classic Tomato Soup (page 120) because making the soup is a bit of work, so making a double batch is efficient. Enjoy Round One on the day you make the soup, then freeze the rest for an instant dinner a couple of months later. You'll be glad you did.

I use bone-in, skin-on chicken because I like the flavor of the chicken fat that renders from the skin during simmering, but boneless, skinless thighs are less fussy and just fine.

MAKES ABOUT 3½ QUARTS (3.3 L)

Extra-virgin olive oil

1 pound (450 g) bone-in, skin-on chicken thighs or ¾ pound (340 g) boneless, skinless chicken thighs

3 medium fresh mild green chiles, such as Anaheim, poblano, or Hatch, seeded and cut into ½-inch (1.25 cm) pieces (about 1 cup/100 g)

3 tablespoons finely chopped fresh ginger

1 jalapeño, seeded and finely chopped

Kosher salt

2 teaspoons ground turmeric

2 teaspoons ground coriander

2 teaspoons ground cumin

1 teaspoon ground cardamom

⅛ teaspoon chile flakes, plus more to taste

2 recipes Classic Tomato Soup (page 120)

One 13.5-ounce (400 ml) can unsweetened coconut milk

½ small bunch cilantro, stems left whole and leaves roughly chopped

1 lime, halved

In a large soup pot or Dutch oven, heat a glug of olive oil over medium-high heat. Pat the chicken pieces dry and add to the pot. Brown both sides of the chicken, adjusting the heat so you can get a nice amount of browning without burning the juices in the bottom of the pot. Take your time with this step; you only want to brown the surface and develop some meaty flavor, which should take about 4 minutes per side (less for boneless, skinless thighs). The chicken will cook fully as it simmers in the soup.

Remove the chicken and set aside. Pour off all but about 2 tablespoons of grease (or pour off all the grease and add 2 tablespoons olive oil). Add the mild chiles, ginger, jalapeño, and a pinch of salt. Cook until the chiles start to soften and sweeten, about 4 minutes. Add the turmeric, coriander, cumin, cardamom, and chile flakes and cook for another minute to bloom the spices.

Add the tomato soup, coconut milk, and cilantro stems and return the browned chicken to the pot. Simmer, partially covered, until the chicken is fully cooked and very tender, about 40 minutes (to confirm, take out a piece and cut into it).

Remove the chicken, and when it's cool enough to handle, shred or cut it into bite-size pieces (discard the skin and bones, if using bone-in, skin-on). Remove the cilantro stems (tongs make this easy); it's okay if a few remain.

Return the chicken to the soup and add a big squeeze of lime juice. Taste and adjust the seasoning with more salt, chile flakes, and/or lime juice. Finish with the chopped cilantro leaves and serve hot.

PASSATA

Passata is a mellifluous word that usually means a puree of lightly cooked tomatoes, though some people make passata without cooking. Both versions are components you would make during peak tomato season and then preserve in jars for use later in the year.

I don't make either version, for no reason other than a preference for chunky sauces rather than smooth ones. I also don't actually can tomatoes very often, preferring to make a basic tomato sauce and freeze it or freeze raw tomatoes to use in various ways later, and then use store-bought canned tomatoes during the off-season.

You will find commercial products labeled "passata" and "strained tomatoes"; Pomì and Mutti are two imported brands with wide distribution. Some brands have a more cooked flavor than others, but all are cooked to some degree, because the canning or other packaging process involves heating, as does home-canning.

Despite its not being part of my tomato-preserving routine, passata is a useful pantry item and a good way to capture your harvest.

To make your own passata, cut your tomatoes into large chunks, pile them into a large pot, and bring the fruit to a simmer over medium-high heat, stirring frequently with a long utensil so you can reach the bottom of the pot. You can add a bit of water to the pot to get things moving, if you like.

Once the tomatoes are slightly broken down (skins are curling, flesh is losing its shape), let the tomatoes cool and then put them through a food mill to remove the skins and seeds. Alternatively, puree them in a blender or food processor and then strain. Can the passata in pint or quart (500 ml or 1 L) jars, following a good canning guide. Your canned passata should be good for 1 year.

Tomato Pastas and Risottos

Sheet-Pan Spaghetti Sauce

This recipe doesn't fit the image of Nonna's red sauce bubbling on the stove, but it is equally satisfying, especially because it requires so little work. You roughly chop the ingredients, spread them on the sheet pan, and anoint them with olive oil, and into the oven they go to roast and sweeten. The final step takes place in the blender, where you'll whiz the ingredients until they have the texture you want—from super chunky all the way to smooth; for silky, however, you'll need to strain the sauce.

Because the method is mostly hands-off, however, you have slightly less control than with a more traditional stovetop sauce. You will need to monitor the vegetables to make sure they lightly caramelize without their juices actually burning, which would make your sauce bitter. If you do get a bit of burning, though, don't worry; simply don't scrape the dark juices into the blender.

MAKES ABOUT 2 CUPS (480 ML); ENOUGH FOR 1 POUND (450 G) PASTA

1½ pounds (680 g) tomatoes, cored and cut into chunks

1 large red bell pepper, halved (optional)

1 small onion (90 g), thickly sliced

3 garlic cloves, roughly chopped

A few sprigs fresh thyme and/or rosemary

¼ cup (60 ml) extra-virgin olive oil, plus more to taste

⅛ teaspoon chile flakes, plus more to taste

Kosher salt and freshly ground black pepper

Small handful of fresh flat-leaf parsley, basil, and/or oregano leaves (if using only oregano, use just a few leaves, as it can be strong)

Water, broth, or Tomato Water (page 70), if needed

Lemon juice, if needed

Pinch of sugar, if needed

NOTE

As the name indicates, this sauce is a perfect match for spaghetti or other long noodles such as linguine or bucatini. It's also excellent as a topping for grilled pizza, bruschetta, or slices of roasted eggplant.

Preheat the oven to 400°F (200°C).

Pile the tomatoes, bell pepper (if using), onion, garlic, and thyme on a sheet pan, pour the oil over everything, and scoot things around to mix and coat the ingredients. Season with the chile flakes, 1 teaspoon salt, and many twists of black pepper. Toss again to mix.

Roast in the hot oven until everything is hot and bubbling and the onion is soft, 30 to 45 minutes. Take care not to let the juices burn—stir the vegetables a few times during cooking, and if it looks like the juices are getting quite dark, reduce the oven temperature a bit. Don't let any stray pieces of vegetables migrate away from the larger mass, because they can burn when unprotected from the heat by the other ingredients. When everything is sizzling and smells great, take the pan from the oven and leave until cool enough to touch.

Pluck off as many tomato skins as you have the patience for. It's fine to leave them all, but losing a few will create a nicer final texture. Pull out and discard any tough herb stems; the leaves are fine.

Transfer the ingredients to a blender, and if the juices on the sheet pan don't look burned, dissolve them with a bit of water and add to the blender (if they're too dark, they'll be bitter; taste to decide). Add the fresh herbs.

continues

Blend the ingredients, scraping down the sides of the blender as needed. Stop blending when the texture looks good to you. You can keep things quite chunky or go all the way to smooth, finessing the texture even more by pushing the puree through a sieve, if you like. If the sauce is too thick, add a small amount of water, broth, or tomato water.

Taste and adjust the seasoning with more olive oil, salt, black pepper, chile flakes, and/or a few drops of lemon juice and/or a pinch of sugar.

The sauce will keep well in the fridge for up to 4 days. Reheat when you're ready to use it on pasta, polenta, or whatever the final destination is.

THE BEST SAUCE-TO-PASTA RATIO

In this chapter, you'll find a selection of my favorite tomato-based sauces (plus one pesto), which are all perfect for pasta. But the sauces are also excellent on polenta, in lasagna, for braising thick pork chops, and for smothering swordfish steaks. In other words, spaghetti sauce isn't just for spaghetti.

That is why I've listed the recipe yields in cups rather than number of servings, and why I'm suggesting pasta shapes that pair well with the sauces but not uniting the sauce with the noodles as part of the recipe.

But, of course, pasta will be a primary destination for the sauces, so here's a rule of thumb for the sauce-to-noodle ratio.

FOR TOMATO-BASED SAUCES

1½ to 2 cups (360 to 480 ml) of sauce will dress 1 pound (450 g) of pasta, with the lower amount reflecting a more restrained, Italian approach and the higher amount reflecting a lots-of-sauce approach.

FOR PESTO SAUCES

About 1 cup (240 ml) sauce will dress 1 pound (450 g) of pasta. You use less pesto than tomato sauce, as pesto is intense and doesn't contain chunks of tomato or vegetables, which add volume.

TIPS FOR SAUCING ANY PASTA

The best way to get the perfect sauce consistency is to use some of the pasta cooking water. Heat your sauce in a pan that can hold all the pasta. Keep the sauce warm while you cook your pasta until just al dente, according to the package instructions. When it's almost ready to drain, scoop out about 1 cup (240 ml) of the water, which will be salty and slightly starchy. You probably won't use the full cup unless you're making pasta for a crowd, but you might as well have plenty.

Drain the pasta, add it to the sauce, and add a few spoonfuls of pasta water. Cook for a few seconds, tossing the noodles until they're nicely coated and have soaked up some of the sauce. Taste and adjust with more pasta water and cheese (if using) until the consistency is creamy and emulsified and the pasta is a perfect al dente and nicely integrated with the sauce. Serve right away.

Fresh Tomato Marinara Sauce (with a Secret Ingredient)

"Marinara sauce" has become a catchall phrase to mean any kind of tomato sauce that doesn't have meat in it, but it really means something specific: a quickly made sauce of fresh tomatoes, garlic, olive oil, and maybe basil . . . at least this is how a few Italian experts describe it. I'm sure I'll hear some differing opinions!

Regardless of historical accuracy, this type of sauce is a delight and a perfect destination for peak-season tomatoes. In fact, don't make it with so-so tomatoes; use them in something that cooks longer and involves more supporting ingredients.

Capture the juices as you're cutting the tomatoes and—here's the secret ingredient—if you have tomato water in your fridge or freezer, as I hope you do, add it and let it reduce as the sauce cooks, which will intensify the bright essence of tomato. As for peeling the tomatoes, for most recipes I don't, but in this instance, peeling them will make the texture of the sauce light and lovely.

MAKES ABOUT 2 CUPS (480 ML); ENOUGH FOR 1 POUND (450 G) PASTA

¼ cup (60 ml) extra-virgin olive oil

3 or 4 garlic cloves, smashed

1 cup Tomato Water (page 70; optional, but it makes a difference)

2 pounds (900 g) tomatoes, peeled if you feel like it (see page 24), cut into smallish chunks

1 small dried red chile, such as chile de árbol or cayenne, or a pinch of chile flakes

Kosher salt

A few fresh basil leaves, even fewer fresh oregano leaves (they are assertive), or ¼ teaspoon dried oregano

Freshly ground black pepper, lemon juice, and/or sugar, if needed

NOTE

I usually serve this with something long and classic, such as spaghetti, linguine, or angel hair, showered with plenty of Parmigiano-Reggiano.

In a large skillet, heat the olive oil over medium heat. Add the garlic and cook until it's very soft, fragrant, and nicely golden brown but not dark, about 4 minutes, breaking up the smashed cloves a bit with your spatula as they cook.

If using tomato water, add it now, increase the heat to medium-high, and simmer until the tomato water has reduced by about half. Add the tomatoes, whole chile (or chile flakes), and 1 teaspoon salt. Adjust the heat so the tomatoes simmer vigorously and cook until the juices have reduced, the tomato chunks have partially disintegrated, and the flavor is concentrated and sweet but still with a freshness, about 10 minutes. Scrape the bottom and sides of the pan a lot as you cook down the tomatoes.

Add the basil and continue cooking for about 5 minutes to perfume the sauce. Remove the whole chile (if used) and the basil leaves (if still intact). If you see any big chunks of garlic, either smash them so they blend into the sauce or remove them, too. Taste the sauce and add more salt and/or a bit of pepper, lemon juice, and/or sugar to balance the flavors.

This sauce is best eaten right after you make it, but you can keep it in the fridge for 1 or 2 days if you need to; loosen it with a few drops of water or tomato water as you reheat it.

Foundational Tomato Sauce

This is the tomato sauce I've been making for years. I may tinker around the edges each time I make it—celery or fennel? chile flakes or hot sauce?—but I find the basic sauce not only delicious but also so versatile that I can use it for pasta, polenta, lasagna, and braises, and it's a perfect platform for improvisation. The sauce freezes beautifully, so make a double or triple batch and divide it into portions.

The key to this sauce is the transformation of the tomatoes from acidic to deeply sweet and savory. This happens with time, so be patient and cook your sauce until it reaches this state. Even with plenty of cooking, however, some tomatoes stay on the sharp side, so I give suggestions for dialing in the final flavors.

MAKES ABOUT 6 CUPS (1.5 L);
ENOUGH FOR 3 POUNDS (1.35 KG)
PASTA

½ cup (120 ml) extra-virgin olive oil

1½ cups (225 g) finely chopped onion

½ cup (65 g) coarsely grated or finely chopped carrot

½ cup (65 g) coarsely grated or finely chopped celery

Kosher salt and freshly ground black pepper

⅛ teaspoon chile flakes, plus more to taste

2 tablespoons tomato paste (optional)

2 or 3 garlic cloves, finely chopped

Two 28-ounce (794 g) cans whole peeled tomatoes, and the juices, broken up a bit, or crushed tomatoes

½ cup (15 g) thinly sliced fresh basil leaves or chopped fresh flat-leaf parsley (or a mixture)

1 or 2 sprigs fresh rosemary and/or thyme (optional)

Fresh lemon juice, if needed

Pinch of sugar, if needed

NOTES

- This sauce is so versatile that it works well with most pasta shapes, though I feel it's a bit heavy/chunky for delicate angel hair. Think beyond the noodle, too: use it as a braising liquid (loosened with a bit of water or broth) for a pot roast or thick pork chops or spoon some in the center of a simple risotto, for extra comfort.

- I mostly make this sauce with canned tomatoes, preferring to save fresh tomatoes for marinara, but if you'd like to use fresh tomatoes, use about 5 pounds (2.3 kg) and plan to cook them longer than the time I suggest for canned. Also, this is one place where you should peel the fresh tomatoes.

- The tomato paste is optional because I know not everyone either makes their own or can find it in a tube (hint: the tubes are usually on the top shelf at the grocery store), and there's nothing more annoying than using a half can of tomato paste and having the rest go to waste.

In a large wide heavy saucepan, large Dutch oven, or large deep sauté pan, heat the olive oil over medium heat. Add the onion, carrot, celery, ½ teaspoon salt, several twists of black pepper, and the chile flakes and cook, stirring occasionally, until soft, fragrant, and lightly golden, 10 to 15 minutes; don't let the vegetables actually brown. Add the tomato paste (if using) and cook for another few minutes until the paste has toasted a bit. Add the garlic and cook for another 30 seconds or so (don't let it brown).

Add the tomatoes and herbs and bring the tomatoes to a simmer. Reduce the heat to maintain a low simmer and cook uncovered, stirring and scraping the bottom and sides of the pan every once in a while—and of course tasting as you go—until the sauce is reduced, glistening with oil, and concentrated in flavor. This should take 40 to 50 minutes, longer if using fresh tomatoes. Taste again and adjust the flavor balance: a squeeze of lemon juice if the sauce seems flat, a pinch of sugar if it's sharp, and more salt and/or chile flakes as needed.

Refrigerate in an airtight container for up to 1 week or freeze (in one or more freezer bags) for up to 3 months.

TOASTING TOMATO PASTE

A little can of tomato paste doesn't present itself as a power player in the kitchen, but when it's handled correctly, just a few spoonfuls can bring a remarkable depth of flavor to your dishes.

Whether using tomato paste from a can or tube or your own stash of conserva (see page 197), the key is to toast it as you add it to your dish.

Most recipes have you add the tomato paste to the other aromatics—sautéed onion, garlic, carrots, etc.—and then immediately add your tomatoes. Instead, once your aromatic vegetables are close to ready, add the tomato paste and immediately spread it around the surface of the pan using a spatula or wooden spoon. If your pan is oily, the paste might slip around a bit, but eventually it will spread out into a thin layer. Now cook, stirring and scraping a bit, caramelizing it as deeply as you can without burning. The color will darken from bright red to deep brick, which means the flavors are deepening as well.

Tomato Sauce with Mushrooms and Sweet Peppers

This recipe is a great one to make when navigating between vegetarians and meat lovers at the same meal. The sauce is meatless (and can be vegan if you omit the butter and Worcestershire sauce), yet the mushrooms create a kind of bass-note meatiness, as they are the ultimate umami bombs. Basic white or cremini mushrooms will bring plenty of mushroom character, but, of course, if you find yourself with fresh wild mushrooms, use them here.

MAKES ABOUT 4 CUPS (1 L); ENOUGH FOR 2 POUNDS (900 G) PASTA

½ recipe Foundational Tomato Sauce (page 136); about 3 cups (720 ml)

Extra-virgin olive oil

12 ounces (340 g) white, cremini, and/or wild mushrooms, stems trimmed and cut into roughly ½-inch (1.5 cm) chunks

Kosher salt and freshly ground black pepper

2 tablespoons (30 g) butter

1 red bell pepper (or about an equivalent amount of other sweet red peppers, such as lipstick or Jimmy Nardello), thinly sliced

⅛ teaspoon chile flakes or Aleppo pepper, plus more to taste

2 teaspoons fresh thyme (or a big sprig)

1 teaspoon Worcestershire sauce

Pinch of sugar

Big squeeze of lemon juice

NOTE

Serve this sauce with big hollow noodles such as rigatoni or paccheri, which are good at capturing chunks of mushroom in each bite. For a chicken cacciatore–type stew, brown some chicken thighs, pour on some sauce, and simmer until they are fully tender.

In a large saucepan, gently heat the tomato sauce while you prepare the other ingredients.

In a large skillet, heat a thin film of olive oil over medium-high heat. Add the mushrooms, spreading them in a single layer. (To avoid crowding, cook in batches.) Season with a big pinch of salt and a few twists of black pepper and cook undisturbed until the undersides are nicely browned, 3 to 5 minutes. Flip them and cook, stirring frequently, until they have released their liquid and are browned all over, another 7 to 8 minutes. Toss in the butter and cook until nicely browned and fragrant, another minute or two. Add to the tomato sauce.

If the surface of your skillet is getting dark, rinse and wipe it out so you don't introduce burned flavors to your sauce. Return the pan to the heat, add a glug of olive oil, and add the red pepper, another pinch of salt, the chile flakes, several twists of black pepper, and the thyme. Sauté over medium-high heat for a minute or so, then reduce the heat to medium-low and continue to cook the peppers more gently until they are very sweet and tender (taste one), with a hint of browning around the edges, 15 to 20 minutes. Add to the tomato sauce.

Bring the sauce to a simmer and stir in the Worcestershire sauce, sugar, and lemon juice. Simmer gently for another 15 to 20 minutes. If the sauce seems too thick, loosen it with a bit of water. Taste and adjust with more of any of those seasonings and more salt, pepper, and/or chile flakes. Refrigerate in an airtight container for up to 1 week or freeze for up to 3 months.

Slightly Excessive Meat Sauce

My intention with this sauce was to create layers of meaty flavor, which is why the recipe uses three types of meat, plus broth. To streamline things, you could drop any of the meats and increase the quantity of the other two, though too much pancetta might make the texture a bit chewy.

MAKES ABOUT 4½ CUPS (1 L); ENOUGH FOR AT LEAST 2 POUNDS (900 G) PASTA

Extra-virgin olive oil

2 ounces (60 g) pancetta, finely chopped (freeze it briefly to make it easier to chop)

4 ounces (115 g) sweet or hot Italian sausage, casings removed if using links

4 ounces (115 g) ground beef, preferably grass-fed, 80% lean

½ recipe Foundational Tomato Sauce (page 136); about 3 cups (720 ml)

1 cup (240 ml) homemade chicken, turkey, or beef broth or canned low-sodium chicken broth

1 sprig fresh rosemary

1 bay leaf

½ teaspoon Worcestershire sauce

Kosher salt and freshly ground black pepper, if needed

Hot sauce, if needed

Lemon juice, if needed

Sugar, if needed

NOTE

Serve this on pappardelle, which is a classic pasta partner for a meaty ragù, or go super hearty and fold some big white gigante beans and sautéed cabbage into the sauce.

In a large saucepan or deep skillet (big enough to hold all the tomato sauce), heat a glug of olive oil over medium-high heat. Add the pancetta and cook, stirring occasionally, until the fat is rendered and the pancetta is golden brown but not crispy, 4 to 5 minutes. Add the sausage and ground beef and cook, breaking up the meat with a wooden spoon or spatula, until the pink is gone (but don't let the meat get crusty), 3 to 4 minutes. If a lot of fat has accumulated in the pan, pour some off, but leave 2 to 3 tablespoons, which will make the sauce more flavorful.

Stir in the tomato sauce, broth, rosemary, bay leaf, and Worcestershire sauce. Cover, reduce the heat to maintain a gentle simmer, and cook, stirring and scraping the pan fairly frequently, for about 30 minutes to let the meats soften and the flavors infuse into the tomato sauce.

Uncover and continue to simmer until the sauce is very concentrated and glistening with oil, another 5 minutes or so. Taste and adjust the flavor balance if needed with salt and pepper, a shake of hot sauce, a few drops of lemon juice, and/or a pinch of sugar to create the right savory-sweet balance.

Refrigerate in an airtight container for up to 1 week or freeze for up to 3 months.

All the Salty Things Tomato Sauce

I like briny things—capers, olives, anchovies—so this sauce is just my cup of tea. But you should add only what you like in order to make a sauce that's bright and assertive and to your taste. And at least a little bit salty.

MAKES ABOUT 4 CUPS (1 L); ENOUGH FOR AT LEAST 2 POUNDS (900 G) PASTA

Extra-virgin olive oil

A lot of oil-packed anchovy fillets, well drained (I use a whole can, but you might start with 4 or 5 fillets)

1 tablespoon finely chopped drained oil-packed hot red peppers, such as Calabrian chiles or Mama Lil's brand

2 or 3 garlic cloves, finely chopped

½ recipe Foundational Tomato Sauce (page 136); about 3 cups (720 ml)

¾ cup (80 g) chopped pitted Kalamata olives or other pitted olives that you like

¼ cup (50 g) drained brined capers (or salted capers that have been soaked and rinsed a few times), roughly chopped

½ cup (15 g) coarsely chopped fresh flat-leaf parsley

½ teaspoon lightly packed finely grated lemon zest

Kosher salt and freshly ground black pepper, if needed

Pinch of sugar, if needed

Lemon juice, if needed

NOTE

Serve this with a ridged or curly pasta that will catch the briny bits, such as fusilli, penne, or perhaps a shell. The sauce is delicious on grilled fish, especially a thick swordfish steak.

In a large saucepan or deep skillet (big enough to hold all the tomato sauce), heat a glug of olive oil over medium heat. Add the anchovies, hot peppers, and garlic and cook until sizzling, about 30 seconds, stirring a few times to break up the anchovies and taking care not to let the garlic get dark.

Add the tomato sauce, along with the olives, capers, parsley, and lemon zest. Simmer gently for about 15 minutes to blend all the flavors. Taste and adjust with a little salt (I doubt you'll need it), black pepper, sugar, and/or lemon juice if needed.

Refrigerate in an airtight container for up to 1 week or freeze for up to 3 months.

Creamy Tomato Sauce
(with or without Vodka)

While this recipe isn't exactly the same as the popular penne à la vodka, it shares the concept: tomato sauce enriched with cream and given a certain something with the addition of vodka. Or not.

In researching the function of the vodka in this sauce, I haven't come across an explanation that I find fully convincing. The most scientific ones purport that the vodka releases certain alcohol-soluble flavor compounds in the sauce, but other food writers lean more toward the "I don't know, but I like it" explanation. I fall into that camp, and I am hard-pressed to describe the difference in flavor if the vodka is omitted. Vodka adds . . . an edge? What seems to matter most is the effect of the cream on the tomato sauce: a silky richness that is undeniably delicious.

MAKES ABOUT 3 CUPS (720 ML); ENOUGH FOR ABOUT 1½ POUNDS (680 G) PASTA

Extra-virgin olive oil

2 tablespoons tomato paste

½ recipe Foundational Tomato Sauce (page 136); about 3 cups (720 ml)

½ cup (120 ml) heavy cream or crème fraîche

3 tablespoons vodka (optional)

Kosher salt and freshly ground black pepper

Hot sauce, if needed

NOTE

Serve this sauce with penne, obviously, but I also like it on simple cheese ravioli or layered into a lasagna.

In a large saucepan or deep skillet (big enough to hold all the tomato sauce), heat a small glug of olive oil over medium-high heat. Add the tomato paste and cook, smearing and scraping it in the pan so it darkens and toasts a bit. Add the tomato sauce, stirring to dissolve the tomato paste, and cook just long enough to warm everything up.

Transfer the sauce to a blender and blend until completely smooth, then return to the pan. If you want to get fanatical about it, strain it as you pour from blender to pan.

Add the cream and vodka (if using) and bring the sauce to a simmer. Cook until the raw cream flavor has mellowed and reduced a bit and the alcohol has dissipated. Taste for seasoning, adding salt, pepper, and/or a few drops of hot sauce as needed.

Refrigerate in an airtight container for up to 5 days.

Tomato Leaf and Basil Pesto

Is it silly to put tomato leaves into pesto when there are plenty of delicious leafy herbs already perfect for it? Maybe, but I find it quietly thrilling to consume a part of the tomato plant that most people don't even know is edible, one that gives me so much pleasure through its compelling fragrance (see page 61). And when you have a lot of tomato plants in your garden, you'll have a lot more tomato leaves than basil leaves.

Choose only tender, moist leaves, balancing their flavor here with basil and/or other tender herbs such as parsley, mint, or cilantro; tomato leaves alone would be too strong. The cheese is optional; make pesto with no cheese when you want full-on green, grassy flavors without the richness of Parmigiano, as for, perhaps, a salad with tomatoes and burrata, where there's already plenty of dairy goodness.

MAKES ABOUT 1 CUP (300 G) WITH THE CHEESE ADDED; ENOUGH FOR 1 POUND (450 G) PASTA

2 cups (100 g) lightly packed tender tomato leaves (strip away any tough stems)

1 cup (30 g) lightly packed fresh basil, flat-leaf parsley, or mint leaves (or a mix)

¼ cup (35 g) pine nuts

1 or 2 small garlic cloves, smashed

Kosher salt

½ teaspoon lightly packed finely grated lemon zest

½ cup (120 ml) extra-virgin olive oil, plus more as needed

½ cup (50 g) freshly grated Parmigiano-Reggiano cheese (optional)

NOTE

Serve this pesto with its classic partner, linguine, or another delicate long noodle, such as angel hair. Or look for corzetti, an embossed wafer of pasta traditionally served in Liguria with pesto. I also like to spread this pesto, with or without the cheese, on salmon fillets before I roast them in a hot oven, and it makes a fragrant filling for stuffed chicken breasts.

In a food processor, combine the tomato leaves, basil, pine nuts, garlic, 1 teaspoon salt, and the lemon zest and pulse a few times to make a coarse puree.

With the machine running, pour in the olive oil through the feed tube. Stop when you've added all the oil.

Scrape down the sides of the processor, add the Parmigiano, if using, and pulse for another few seconds to blend everything. I like a slightly coarse pesto, but if you'd like it smoother, process until the consistency looks good to you.

Taste (watch out for that processor blade!) and adjust with more olive oil and/or salt, if you like. Use right away or scrape into a jar, float a thin layer of olive oil on the surface, and store in the refrigerator for a day or two. You can freeze the pesto in a zip-top bag with all the air pushed out for up to 3 months.

Flash-Sautéed Cherry Tomatoes, Lemon, and Tuna on Angel Hair Pasta

This is the ultimate weeknight meal—it's quick to make, it uses only two pans, and most of the ingredients are likely in your pantry or fridge. In the summer, I get the tomatoes right from my garden, but you can make this dish in non-tomato season, as it works just fine with cherry or grape tomatoes from the grocery store.

The idea is to sauté the tomatoes over lively heat until they burst and release their juices, which reduce into a nice coating consistency. Some tomatoes need a bit of encouragement, so if they're not bursting after a few minutes of cooking, pierce them with a knife and squish them with a spatula.

I make this dish with canned tuna because I love it so much, but you can skip the protein or swap in something else. Just be sure that either your add-ins will be cooked in the 6 to 10 minutes the tomatoes need or that you give them a head start.

SERVES 2

3 tablespoons extra-virgin olive oil

4 cups cherry tomatoes (about 1¼ pounds/565 g)

Kosher salt

1 large garlic clove, finely chopped

⅛ teaspoon chile flakes, plus more to taste

1 teaspoon packed finely grated lemon zest

1 teaspoon fresh lemon juice, plus more to taste

One 5-ounce (142 g) can light tuna in oil (see Note), drained and broken up into chunks

1 teaspoon (5 g) cold butter

8 ounces (225 g) angel hair pasta

¼ cup (7 g) roughly chopped fresh basil (or a mix of basil and cilantro)

NOTE

I prefer "light" tuna over white or albacore, which always seems dry and tasteless. My favorite brand is Genova, which has yellowfin and albacore, both packed in olive oil. Choose the yellowfin.

Bring a large pot of water to a boil for the pasta.

In a large skillet, heat the olive oil over medium-high heat until very hot. Add the tomatoes and cook until they begin to collapse and their juices run and start to thicken. (Be careful, because the oil and juice will spatter.) This should take 6 to 10 minutes. If you have big, stubborn tomatoes, you may need to crush them a bit with a spatula or pierce them with a knife.

Season generously with salt, add the garlic and chile flakes, and cook for 30 seconds or so, then take the pan off the heat and fold in the lemon zest, lemon juice, tuna, and butter. Keep the sauce warm while you cook the pasta.

Once the pasta water boils, add about 2 tablespoons salt, then add the pasta, stir, and cook until just 1 minute shy of al dente according to the package directions (which for angel hair, might be only 2 minutes). Just before the pasta is ready, scoop out about ½ cup (120 ml) of the cooking water and set aside.

Drain the pasta thoroughly and add it to the skillet. Toss to coat the pasta well, splashing in a bit of the reserved pasta water to create a creamy consistency and to finish cooking the noodles. Taste and adjust with more salt, chile flakes, and/or lemon juice. Arrange in serving bowls and top with the fresh herbs.

Pasta with No-Cook Tomato Sauce with Feta, Mint, and Parsley

I'm not a fan of pasta salads, probably because I made too many as a caterer back in the late 1980s (so many Martha Stewart tortellini skewers!), but a pasta dish that is meant to be served at room temperature can make entertaining easier. When friends come over in the summer, my preferred menu is something cooked on the grill served with an array of room-temperature vegetable salads and pasta or grain dishes, and this is often one of them.

The key is using a truly ripe and flavorful tomato, because you're not going to concentrate its flavor by cooking it, as you might in another dish. If your raw tomatoes aren't all they should be, try this dish with one of the roasted-tomato options (see pages 48, 151, or 165).

SERVES 3 OR 4

1 pound (450 g) tomatoes, cored and cut into ½-inch (1.25 cm) cubes

1 small garlic clove, very finely chopped or grated

Kosher salt

8 ounces (225 g) pasta (pretty much any shape will work)

4 ounces (115 g) feta, preferably Valbreso, a creamy French sheep's-milk cheese, cut into ½-inch (1.25 cm) cubes

½ cup (90 g) pitted interesting olives, such as Kalamata, Castelvetrano, or Lucques, or a mix, roughly chopped

½ cup (15 g) lightly packed mixed fresh mint leaves and flat-leaf parsley leaves and tender stems, roughly chopped

Grated zest from 1 lemon

Freshly ground black pepper

Pinch of Aleppo pepper or cayenne

Extra-virgin olive oil

Put the tomatoes and garlic into a sieve set over a bowl to catch the juices. Sprinkle with about ½ teaspoon salt, then toss to mix. Leave to drain for about 20 minutes. (Macerating the garlic with the tomatoes will soften its raw edge.)

While the tomatoes are draining, arrange all your ingredients so they're at hand when it's time to toss the pasta.

Bring a large pot of water to a boil and add about 2 tablespoons salt. Add the pasta and cook until al dente according to the package directions; start testing for doneness 1 or 2 minutes before the specified time.

When the pasta is done, scoop out about ½ cup (120 ml) of the cooking water, then drain the pasta thoroughly and return it to the pot. Add the drained tomatoes, feta, olives, herbs, and lemon zest. Season with a bit more salt, some generous twists of black pepper, and the Aleppo pepper.

Pour ¼ cup (60 ml) olive oil into the pot. Toss to blend, adding a few spoonfuls of the collected tomato juices to keep things loose and to emulsify with the olive oil so the pasta is cloaked in a creamy sauce rather than just an oily one. If you've added all the tomato juices and the pasta still seems dry, add a few spoonfuls of the reserved cooking water.

Taste and adjust the seasoning. The dish is meant to be served at warm room temperature, not hot, so don't stress about keeping the noodles piping hot, but try not to refrigerate them. If you need to make this way ahead, keep it in the fridge, but give it a good 30 minutes at room temperature to warm up before serving.

BLASTED CHERRY TOMATOES

When your cherry tomato plants are in their glory, it's hard to keep up with them, so set a few aside for a salad or snacking that day, throw a few in the freezer, and fill a sheet pan with the rest and blast them in the oven, to be used over the next couple of days. These blasted tomatoes are quick to make and super versatile, but they don't freeze well because they will lose their shape, so they're better as a make-and-eat-in-one situation. What they lack in shelf life they make up for in curb appeal, especially when you use a mix of colors and shapes. What could be prettier than yellow, red, orange, and green tomatoes, glossed with olive oil and browned by the oven, tumbling across your burrata or polenta?

Managing the Variables

As with any high-temperature cooking, things move fast and you won't have a lot of time for correction if something's heading in the wrong direction. The main thing to look out for is burning juices. Most cherry tomatoes will start giving off juice early in roasting, so you'll have a deep enough layer of juice that it will simply reduce and caramelize rather than burn, but if you see that a few lonely juices are starting to get very dark, pour a few spoonfuls of water into the pan as protection.

The other variable to manage is simply when to stop roasting. You want to take the tomatoes far enough that they gain some color and depth of flavor but not so far that they completely collapse and turn to mush. Again, taking a quick peek through the oven door every few minutes is the best way to assure blasted but not incinerated.

BLASTED CHERRY TOMATOES

MAKES ABOUT 2 POUNDS (900 G), PLUS SOME JUICE

About 3½ pounds (1.6 kg) mixed cherry tomatoes, ideally including Sungolds, halved if large

½ cup (120 ml) extra-virgin olive oil

1 teaspoon kosher salt

A few fresh thyme and rosemary leaves (optional)

Preheat the oven to 450°F (230°C).

Remove any leaves from the tomatoes, pile them onto a sheet pan large enough to hold them in one layer, such as one that measures 13 by 18 inches (33 by 45 cm). Add the olive oil, salt, and herbs (if using) and shimmy the pan to distribute the ingredients.

Roast until the tomatoes are lightly blistered and browned, split, but not completely collapsed into a puree, about 25 minutes. You may need to pour off some of the juices during cooking if they threaten to overflow. If the juice looks like it's starting to burn in spots, either rotate your pan so it flows more evenly or add a few spoonfuls of water.

Let the tomatoes cool and then either transfer them, with the juice, to a covered container or drain off most of the juice to cook down and use as a syrup and store the tomatoes and juice separately. They will keep nicely in the fridge for up to 5 days. I don't generally freeze these because their texture is so fragile that they end up mushy after thawing, the result being a tasty mush that you could toss into a soup, stew, or a pot of beans; or you can puree the frozen tomatoes and use as a pasta sauce. So if you have an overabundance of cherry tomatoes, blasting and freezing is a fine way to preserve them.

Good Things to Do with Blasted Cherry Tomatoes

Use as a bruschetta or pizza topping; toss with pasta, shrimp, and feta; fold into wild rice or other grains; chill and toss into a green salad; chop and add to salsa.

Penne with Blasted Cherry Tomatoes, Fennel, and Salami

This dish is like an Italian sub in pasta form, albeit without the red wine vinegar dressing. I make it with Blasted Cherry Tomatoes, but if you don't already have a batch, no worries; you can cook them as you cook the fennel.

SERVES 4

1¾ to 2 pounds (790 to 900 g) fennel (1 very large or 2 medium bulbs), stalks trimmed off, bulb halved lengthwise and cored

Extra-virgin olive oil

Kosher salt and freshly ground black pepper

Chile flakes or Aleppo pepper

About 1½ cups (600 g) Blasted Cherry Tomatoes (page 151) or 1 pint (340 g) cherry tomatoes, halved

8 ounces (225 g) penne or other short pasta

4 ounces (115 g) fresh mozzarella cheese, coarsely grated or ripped up

¼ cup (60 g) drained and chopped oil-packed mild or hot red peppers, such as Mama Lil's brand

1 ounce (30 g) thinly sliced fennel salami or other salami, cut into thin strips

¼ cup (7 g) roughly chopped fresh flat-leaf parsley or basil

¼ cup (25 g) lightly packed grated Pecorino Romano or Parmigiano-Reggiano cheese, plus (optional) more for serving

Preheat the oven to 425°F (220°C).

Cut the fennel halves crosswise into slices ⅛ inch (3 mm) thick and pile them into a 9-by-13-inch (23 by 33 cm) baking dish or other large shallow dish that will hold them all in one layer; it's okay if the fennel overlaps a bit. Drizzle on about 2 tablespoons olive oil and toss to coat the fennel slices, then season generously with salt, pepper, and chile flakes. Sprinkle on a couple tablespoons of water and roast uncovered until the fennel is soft and starting to brown at the edges, 30 to 40 minutes. Once or twice during roasting, stir and flip the fennel to encourage even cooking.

If you are using Blasted Cherry Tomatoes, just continue cooking the fennel until it's totally soft and starting to caramelize, another 15 minutes or so. If you're using raw cherry tomatoes, scoot the fennel over to one side of the baking dish (it will have shrunk a bit by now), add the tomatoes to the empty space, and season them with salt and pepper. Continue roasting, with an occasional stir, until the tomatoes have collapsed and the juices are bubbling and slightly reduced, another 15 to 20 minutes.

Meanwhile, bring a large pot of water to a boil and add about 2 tablespoons salt. Add the pasta and cook until al dente according to the package directions; start testing for doneness a minute or so before the specified time. When the pasta is done, scoop out about ½ cup (120 ml) of the cooking water, then drain the pasta thoroughly and return it to the pot.

Add the fennel-tomato mixture to the pasta, along with the mozzarella, chopped peppers, salami, and parsley, and toss well. Add the cheese and about ¼ cup (60 ml) of the cooking water and toss again, adding more water as needed until the pasta is very lightly cloaked in a lush sauce and the mozzarella is starting to melt. Season to taste with more salt, black pepper, and/or chile flakes and serve with additional grated cheese, if you like.

Ravioli in Brown-Butter Tomato Sauce

Elegant in its simplicity, this sauce manages to turn just a handful of ingredients into an intriguingly complex partner for pasta. The key ingredient here is butter, and while I often add a bit of solid butter to my final tomato-based pastas to soften any edges of acidity, here you make butter a feature by browning it . . . and using a lot!

   While not as rich as something like a cream sauce, this is still rich, which is why it's perfect for a dinner party first course. The color is beautiful, and you can make the sauce ahead and just rewarm it while the ravioli are cooking. (Pictured on page 129)

MAKES ABOUT 2 CUPS (480 ML) SAUCE; ENOUGH FOR ABOUT 1 POUND (450 G) RAVIOLI; SERVES 6 TO 8 AS A FIRST COURSE

10 tablespoons (145 g) unsalted butter

½ cup (70 g) very finely chopped onion

⅛ teaspoon chile flakes, or to taste

Kosher salt

1 or 2 garlic cloves, chopped

One 28-ounce (794 g) can whole peeled tomatoes and the juices

Lemon juice, if needed

Pinch of sugar, if needed

About 1 pound (450 g) store-bought ravioli of your choice (or homemade, of course!)

Grated Parmigiano-Reggiano cheese (optional), for serving

In a deep skillet or wide saucepan, melt 2 tablespoons (30 g) of the butter over medium heat. Add the onion, chile flakes, and a big pinch of salt and cook until the onion is soft and fragrant but not at all browned, about 4 minutes. Add the garlic and cook for another minute to soften it.

   Add the tomatoes and their juices and break them up with a spatula or wooden spoon. Simmer, stirring frequently so the tomatoes don't stick to the pan, until the sauce has reduced and is thicker and, most important, the flavor has become sweeter and more concentrated, about 25 minutes—taste frequently so you can monitor the transformation of flavor.

   Transfer the sauce to a blender (or a food processor, if yours is large enough) and blend the tomatoes. Strain them back into the skillet through a fine-mesh sieve to capture the seeds and bits of skin; unlike most of my sauces, this one should be silky smooth. Keep the sauce warm.

   With the remaining 8 tablespoons (120 g) butter, make brown butter (see sidebar, opposite). As soon as the butter looks and smells great, pour about half of the melted butter—the liquid butterfat and some of the golden milk solids (unless they look super dark and burned)—into the tomato sauce and whisk to combine. Keep the remaining browned butter warm for garnish, but off the burner so it doesn't continue to cook.

   Taste the tomato sauce and adjust with more salt, chile flakes, a squeeze of lemon, and/or a few sprinkles of sugar if needed. You want the flavor bright and rich at the same time. Keep the sauce warm while you cook the ravioli.

   Bring a large pot of water to a boil and add about 2 tablespoons salt. Add the ravioli and cook according to the package directions. Drain well.

   Reheat the sauce if it cooled and spoon it onto your serving plates. Arrange the ravioli on top and drizzle the remaining brown butter over the ravioli. Serve right away, with grated Parmigiano for diners to add if they like.

HOW TO MAKE BROWN BUTTER

Brown butter is regular butter that you melt and then continue heating until the milk solids in the butter become toasted and golden, creating a rich, nutty flavor.

To make brown butter: Melt your butter in a small saucepan over medium-high heat. Pay attention to the water evaporating, which is what all the bubbling and spitting is about. Once that subsides, reduce the heat to medium-low and continue cooking, swirling the pan every few seconds, until the milk solids on the bottom of the pan begin to turn deep gold and the butter smells really nutty and fragrant. Pay close attention, because the butter can quickly go from nutty to burned. Pull the pan from the burner as soon as you think it's getting close; you can always return the pan to the heat for a few more seconds if needed.

You generally make brown butter just when you are ready to use it, but it can be made ahead and stored in the fridge, where it will solidify. To use, melt gently over low heat.

Tomato Risotto with Summer Veg

Here the tomato flavor comes not from chopped tomatoes but from tomato water, the intensely flavorful liquid that drains from chopped raw tomatoes (see page 68). Tomato water brings incredible flavor to the risotto, and it also means you don't need to add white wine, which is typical in a risotto recipe. The tomato water is so nicely bright, it provides all the acid you'll need.

If you've made tomato water in the summer and frozen it, by all means make this risotto in another season with that season's vegetables. See below for other winning seasonal combinations.

SERVES 2

Extra-virgin olive oil

One 8-ounce (225 g) firm zucchini or other summer squash, cut into ½-inch (1.25 cm) cubes

Kosher salt

Kernels from 1 ear corn

2 cups (480 ml) Tomato Water (page 70), plus plain water as needed

2 tablespoons (30 g) butter

½ cup (75 g) finely chopped onion

Aleppo pepper or chile flakes

½ cup (100 g) risotto rice, such as Arborio or Carnaroli

½ cup (50 g) finely grated Parmigiano-Reggiano cheese

Freshly ground black pepper

In a medium skillet, heat a glug of olive oil over medium-high heat. Add the zucchini and a pinch of salt. Let the zucchini sit undisturbed for about a minute to get a nice browned surface, then flip it over and brown more of the other surfaces. (You don't need to turn every single piece of zucchini, just shake the pan a bit and do your best.)

Cook until the zucchini is browned and slightly tender but not mushy, another minute or so. Add the corn and sauté just to heat through. Set aside.

In a saucepan, bring the tomato water to just below a simmer. You want it to be hot, but you don't want it evaporating and reducing.

In a heavy-bottomed saucepan or deep skillet, melt the butter over medium-high heat. Add the onion and a pinch each of salt and Aleppo pepper and cook, stirring constantly, until the onion is starting to get soft and translucent, 3 to 4 minutes. Add the rice and continue to stir until the grains are glossy and fully coated in the butter, another minute or two.

Ladle in about 1 cup (240 ml) of the warmed tomato water, adjust the heat so that the liquid simmers merrily, and stir the rice gently until the liquid has mostly been absorbed. Add another ½ cup (120 ml) or so and repeat the process, continuing like this until all the tomato water has been absorbed and the rice is fully tender and slightly creamy. You may need to add more liquid, as much as another 1 cup (240 ml). If so, you can use more tomato water if you have it, but plain water is fine.

When the rice is just about tender, fold in the zucchini and corn and cook for a few seconds to warm them. Adjust the consistency of the risotto a final time so that it is fairly wet, adding a few more spoonfuls of water as needed, then stir in half the Parmigiano, which will stiffen the consistency a bit.

Taste and adjust with more salt, black pepper, and/or Aleppo pepper.

Divide between two bowls and serve right away, with the rest of the Parmigiano to pass at the table.

Or Try These Seasonal Ideas

To make this risotto beyond summer (using frozen tomato water), replace the corn and zucchini with peak-season vegetables. Here are some of my favorite combinations.

FALL: Sautéed diced mushrooms and sweet peppers

WINTER: Diced butternut squash and sliced Brussels sprouts, with some chopped pancetta

SPRING: Fava beans, asparagus, and large dice of new/spring onions

Macaroni and Cheese with a Layer of Roasted Tomatoes and Green Chiles

Homemade macaroni and cheese is a near-perfect dish, so why mess with it, you ask? Because you can feel a touch more virtuous when indulging in mac and cheese by adding some vegetables to the mix. Plus the combination of tomatoes, green chiles, and cheese is also near perfect.

I like the slightly husky flavor of poblanos, which usually have a mild to medium spice level, but a mild chile such as Anaheim would also be good, and if you want things hotter, include something higher on the Scoville scale, such as a jalapeño or serrano.

Using roasted tomatoes, which have already had most of their watery juices cooked out, avoids the problem of weepy tomatoes in the casserole and also means the tomatoes will be an intense pop of flavor amid all that mellow cheesy goodness. Make two of these, freeze one unbaked, and then be very glad you did when you come home from a long day and think, "What's for dinner?"

SERVES 4

3 tablespoons butter

3 tablespoons all-purpose flour

2½ cups (600 ml) whole milk

1 cup (115 g) lightly packed grated extra-sharp cheddar cheese

½ cup (60 g) lightly packed grated Gruyère or Comté cheese

¾ cup (75 g) lightly packed finely grated Parmigiano-Reggiano cheese

1 small garlic clove, minced

Kosher salt

¼ teaspoon mustard powder (such as Colman's)

Freshly ground black pepper

Pinch of cayenne or Aleppo pepper

Pinch of freshly grated nutmeg (optional)

In a medium saucepan set over medium-high heat, combine the butter and flour and, as the butter melts, whisk to blend into a paste (called a roux). Cook, whisking a lot, for about 1 minute. This will give the flour a nutty, rather than floury, flavor.

Pull the pan off the heat and pour in about ¼ cup (60 ml) of the milk. Whisk like crazy to form a smooth paste, then whisk in the rest of the milk. Don't stress if you see a few lumps; just whisk a bit more, and they'll eventually surrender and smooth out.

Return the pan to medium heat and bring to a simmer, whisking frequently and making sure to get into the corners of the pan where the thicker sauce can accumulate.

Simmer, whisking frequently, until the sauce is smooth and glossy and no taste of raw flour remains, 8 to 10 minutes. As the sauce simmers, be sure to scrape down the sides of the pan where the sauce builds up and whisk it back into the sauce; otherwise, you will be creating more lumps.

Reduce the heat to low and add the three cheeses. Whisk until completely melted. Add the garlic, ½ teaspoon salt, the mustard powder, quite a few twists of black pepper, cayenne, and nutmeg (if using). Taste and adjust the seasoning. You want the sauce to be assertively flavored, because you'll be pairing it with mild-tasting pasta. Remove from the heat.

continues

continues

8 ounces (225 g) elbow macaroni, penne, or other short pasta

About 1 cup (250 g) roughly chopped Classic Roasted Tomatoes (page 48) or Low and Slow Roasted Plum Tomatoes (page 165)

3 large or 4 smaller poblano chiles, roasted, peeled, seeded, and roughly chopped (to yield about 1 cup/250 g)

Crumb Topping

1 cup (50 g) coarse fresh bread crumbs (you can use panko, but I prefer the lighter crunch you get with fresh)

2 tablespoons (30 g) butter, melted

Preheat the oven to 400°F (200°C).

Bring a large pot of water to a boil and add about 2 tablespoons salt. Add the macaroni, stir, and cook until al dente according to the package directions; start testing for doneness about a minute before the specified time. Drain well, return the macaroni to the pot, add the cheese sauce, and toss to coat evenly. It might seem like there's a lot of sauce, but the pasta will absorb it and the whole dish will thicken up as it bakes and then cools.

Distribute the roasted tomatoes and chiles over the bottom of an 8-inch (20 cm) square—or the equivalent— baking dish. Pour the cheesy macaroni on top.

To make the crumb topping: In a small bowl, toss the bread crumbs with the melted butter. Distribute over the top of the macaroni.

Bake until the surface is browned and bubbling, 20 to 25 minutes. Let rest for about 10 minutes before serving; this rest makes a difference in the final consistency. If you have leftovers, keep them in the fridge for up to 2 days and reheat them gently in a 350°F (175°C) oven.

Pappardelle with Tomato, Tender Leeks, Shrimp, and Brown Butter

"Luxurious" is how to describe this dish, though there's nothing super spendy about it (it would even be good without the shrimp). But something about the silky texture of the tomato confit and melted leeks and the lovely pastel colors make this dish feel a bit special occasion.

You can streamline the slightly complicated cooking method by doing a few steps ahead of time. I call for Low and Slow Roasted Plum Tomatoes here, which you obviously will do ahead, though you can use fresh tomatoes, which you could prep up to a day ahead. A big time-saver would be to also cook the leeks a day ahead. Keep them in the fridge and bring them fully to room temperature before you begin this dish.

SERVES 2 OR 3 AS A MAIN, 4 TO 6 AS A FIRST COURSE

½ pound (225 g) leeks (about 1 medium), roots and top bit of tough green trimmed

7 tablespoons (105 g) unsalted butter

Pinch of chile flakes or Aleppo pepper

Kosher salt

12 ounces (340 g) shrimp (any size), preferably wild, peeled and deveined (if your shrimp are very large, split them in half lengthwise so they'll cook more quickly)

About ½ pound (225 g) Low and Slow Roasted Plum Tomatoes (page 165), or firm-ripe fresh tomatoes, cored, peeled, and seeded

1 or 2 garlic cloves, finely chopped

6 to 8 ounces (170 to 225 g) pappardelle or other long pasta

Split the leeks lengthwise and rinse well, separating the layers in order to get out any hidden grit. Cut crosswise into slices ¼ inch (6 mm) wide. Set aside.

Bring a large pot of water to a boil for the pasta. If it boils before you're finished prepping the other ingredients, just keep it at a simmer.

In a large skillet (one that will hold all the cooked pasta), heat 2 tablespoons (30 g) of the butter over medium heat. Add the chile flakes, leeks, and ½ teaspoon salt. Cook the leeks, stirring frequently, until they are very soft and sweet but not at all browned, 10 to 15 minutes; lower the temperature as needed to avoid browning. If the leeks start to dry out before they're soft, add a few drops of water and cover the pan for a few minutes to create some steam. When the leeks are done, scrape them into a bowl, set aside, and keep warm.

Add another 1 tablespoon butter to the skillet, increase the heat to medium-high, and add the shrimp. Sauté, adjusting the heat as needed to avoid burning any leek juices that may have formed on the bottom of the pan. Cook just until the shrimp are opaque, 3 to 4 minutes, depending on the size of your shrimp. Add the tomatoes and garlic and sauté for a few seconds, just to heat them through (if using fresh tomatoes, cook for a few minutes longer to reduce their juices). Return the leeks to the pan, toss everything together gently, and then set the pan aside, keeping it warm but not cooking it further.

Melt the remaining 4 tablespoons butter in a small saucepan. Set aside and keep warm, but don't let it continue to cook.

continues

continues

1 teaspoon finely grated lemon zest

1 tablespoon fresh lemon juice, plus more to taste

¼ cup (7 g) roughly chopped fresh flat-leaf parsley

Freshly ground black pepper

Add 2 tablespoons salt to the pot of boiling water. Add the pasta and cook until al dente according to the package directions; start testing for doneness a minute or so before the specified time. When it's done, scoop out about ½ cup (120 ml) of cooking water, drain the pasta thoroughly, and add it to the pan with the leeks, shrimp, and tomatoes. Toss gently to mix, scraping the bottom of the pan to dissolve any juices. Put the skillet over low heat so everything stays hot.

Set the pan of melted butter back over medium-high heat and cook, swirling the pan every few seconds, until all the water has evaporated, the milk solids on the bottom of the pan have turned deep gold, and the butter smells really nutty and fragrant. Pay close attention, because the butter can quickly go from nutty to burned.

Immediately pour the brown butter over the pasta, add the lemon zest, lemon juice, and parsley, grind on a few twists of black pepper, and toss, sprinkling in a few spoonfuls of the pasta water if needed to make everything creamy and nice. Taste and add more salt, pepper, and/or lemon juice, if you like.

Distribute among pasta bowls and serve immediately.

LOW AND SLOW ROASTED PLUM TOMATOES

Although these tomatoes are roasted in the oven, they don't have the caramelized nature of Classic Roasted Tomatoes (page 48) but rather are almost chewy and tender, with dense oil-infused flesh. Use plum (Roma) tomatoes for this method, because they are meaty rather than juicy/watery and they hold their shape beautifully, allowing you to slice and dice them into whatever shape your dish requires.

Managing the Variables

This roasted tomato method is easy to manage because plum tomatoes are the most consistent, whether you grow them yourself, buy them from a farmers' market, or pick them up at the grocery store. Plum tomatoes aren't the most exciting, but they are reliably firm, uniform in size, and on the dry side. The only real variable to manage is how to decide when they're done to your liking.

LOW AND SLOW ROASTED PLUM TOMATOES

MAKES ABOUT 2 POUNDS (900 G)

4 pounds (1.8 kg) plum tomatoes

Extra-virgin olive oil

Kosher salt

Preheat the oven to 250°F (120°C).

Slice the tomatoes in half lengthwise. With a paring knife, cut away the little nub in the stem end. With your fingers, scoop out the seeds and, unless your tomatoes are very ripe and red all the way through, cut out the central rib section, which is so often white and hard; discard or add to a batch of Tomato Water (page 70).

Pour a thin layer of olive oil onto a 13-by-18-inch (33 by 45 cm) sheet pan, or use whatever pans you have with low sides that will hold the tomatoes in one snug layer.

Arrange the tomatoes in the pan cut side down, drizzle some olive oil over the top, and sprinkle lightly with salt.

Cook until the tomatoes are very tender and slightly shrunken and the skins are loose and starting to color a bit, about 3 hours. Baste the tomatoes with the pan juices a few times during cooking. If you want a more concentrated flavor, cook longer, but not for so long that the tomatoes start to fall apart.

Let the tomatoes cool slightly, then pull off the skins. Cool completely and store in an airtight container in the refrigerator, topped off by more oil to cover, for up to 1 week, or freeze for up to 3 months.

Good Things to Do with Low and Slow Roasted Plum Tomatoes

Dice and fold into potato, grain, or pasta salads; layer with mozzarella and basil; sandwich between slices of roasted eggplant; top pizza or pissaladière.

Tomato Main Dishes

Chickpea and Tomato Stew with Lots of Greens

Almost everything for this fragrant and slightly addictive stew (which is inspired by chana masala, popular all over the Indian subcontinent) is a common pantry ingredient, so all you need to do for dinner is pick up some nice greens and cilantro.

You can use canned tomatoes, but fresh will work nicely, too, as long as you give them extra time to simmer and become sweet. It's hard to call for a precise amount of the greens, as I find a lot of variation among bunch sizes as well as in the amount of leaf versus stem in the chard or spinach itself. Just remember that the greens, especially the spinach, cook down by a shocking amount, so start with a bit more than you think is right.

SERVES 3 OR 4

1 large bunch Swiss chard or 2 bunches spinach (or a mix)

Coconut oil or extra-virgin olive oil

2 cups (300 g) coarsely chopped onion

2 or 3 fresh mild green chiles, such as Anaheim, seeded and thinly sliced

1 fresh hot green chile, such as jalapeño, seeded and very finely chopped (optional)

A 2-inch (5 cm) piece fresh ginger, peeled and finely chopped

Kosher salt and freshly ground black pepper

5 or 6 garlic cloves, chopped

1 tablespoon garam masala or curry powder

2 teaspoons ground cumin

1 teaspoon ground coriander

1 teaspoon ground turmeric

2 tablespoons tomato paste

Strip or cut away the central ribs from the Swiss chard. Tear or slice the leaves into ribbons and wash well in a few changes of water. Rinse the ribs and chop or slice finely. (If using spinach, just cut away tough stems and discard them and rinse the leaves thoroughly.) Set aside.

In a large pot or Dutch oven, heat a couple tablespoons of coconut oil over medium-high heat. Add the chopped Swiss chard stems (not the spinach), onion, mild green chiles, hot green chile (if using), and ginger. Season with a big pinch of salt and a few twists of black pepper.

Cook, stirring frequently, until the chard stems and aromatic vegetables are fragrant and soft but not actually browned, 7 to 8 minutes. Add the garlic and cook for another minute or so, then stir in the garam masala, cumin, coriander, and turmeric and let cook for a minute or so to bloom.

Clear a space in the center of the pan and dollop in the tomato paste. Cook, spreading and scraping the tomato paste, until it's lightly toasted, about 1 minute. Add the tomatoes and their juices, breaking up the whole tomatoes with your spatula.

Add the chickpeas and coconut milk, stir to combine, and adjust the heat to a lively simmer. Partially cover the pan and cook until the tomatoes are breaking down and the ingredients are getting to know one another. Add the Swiss chard leaves (or spinach), turning them with tongs so they wilt and fit better into the pan.

continues

continues

One 14.5-ounce (411 g) can whole peeled tomatoes and the juices, or 2 large fresh tomatoes, cored, seeded, and chopped

Two 14-ounce (411 g) cans chickpeas, rinsed and drained

One 13.5-ounce (400 ml) can coconut milk

½ small bunch cilantro, roughly chopped, including the stems

Lime wedges

Cooked basmati or other favorite rice, for serving

Plain yogurt, for serving

Add half the chopped cilantro and another big pinch of salt and simmer until the greens are fully tender, 15 to 20 minutes for chard, 10 to 15 for spinach.

Squeeze about 1 tablespoon lime juice into the stew, then taste and dial in the flavors, adding more lime juice, salt, and/or black pepper until the flavor is bright and the creaminess of the coconut milk is apparent but not overly rich.

Shower with the remaining cilantro. Serve with rice and plain yogurt.

Roasted Tomato, Potato, Dill, and Feta Frittata

I love tomatoes and I love eggs, just not together. Plenty of people make egg dishes that include tomatoes and that are no doubt delicious, but something about the way tomatoes render their liquid into the eggs kind of bothers me.

If you use a roasted tomato, from which the excess water has already been cooked out, however, you get deep sweet-savory tomato flavor without the soggy part. Potato, feta, and dill is a classic combo, but try any cheese and herb combination that you like. The tomato part will be delicious no matter what else you use.

SERVES 2 TO 4

12 ounces (340 g) Yukon Gold or other medium-starch potatoes, peeled and cut into ½-inch (1.25 cm) cubes

Kosher salt

Extra-virgin olive oil

1 large onion, thinly sliced

Chile flakes

6 eggs

Freshly ground black pepper

3 tablespoons roughly chopped fresh dill

Generous ½ cup (115 g) roughly chopped Classic Roasted Tomatoes (page 48) or Roasted Canned Tomatoes (page 235)

¾ cup (90 g) crumbled feta, preferably Valbreso, a creamy French sheep's-milk cheese

In a medium saucepan, combine the potatoes, water to cover by 2 inches (5 cm), and about 1 tablespoon salt. Bring to a boil and cook until the potatoes are tender, 12 to 15 minutes. Drain well and set aside.

Preheat the oven to 450°F (230°C).

In a 9- or 10-inch (23 or 25 cm) ovenproof skillet (nonstick is okay), heat a generous glug of oil over medium heat until hot. Add the onion, a pinch of salt, and a pinch of chile flakes and cook, stirring frequently, until the onion is very soft, sweet, and light golden, about 20 minutes. Scrape the bottom of the pan frequently as the onion gets closer to done, because you don't want the sugars to burn.

Transfer the onion to a plate to cool and rinse out the skillet. In a medium bowl, whisk the eggs with 1 teaspoon salt, many twists of black pepper, and the dill. Fold in the cooled onion, potatoes, roasted tomatoes, and feta.

Heat the skillet over medium-high heat and add a nice glug of oil, swirling it so the surface is covered. Pour in the egg mixture, scraping everything out of the bowl with a spatula. Reduce the heat to medium and let the eggs sit undisturbed for a moment or two. Once you see that they are starting to set, carefully slide a silicone spatula around the edges of the eggs to release them from the pan and allow more liquid egg to flow underneath. Let that new layer of egg set up and then repeat the process to build a few layers.

After most of the egg has set, transfer the pan to the oven and bake until any runny egg is cooked through, about 10 minutes. Remove the pan (careful, the handle may be hot), slide a knife around the edge to release the frittata, and slide it onto a cutting board. Let the frittata rest until it's warm but not hot, or serve later at room temperature.

Roasted Fish Fillets with a Jumble of Tomatoes

This is a dish in which the oven does all the work. Once you've chopped your ingredients (and you can be fairly sloppy, er, nonchalant, about that, as precision doesn't matter here), the heat of the oven will transform everything into a bright yet savory sauce. I use cherry tomatoes because I don't want a ton of juice and they aren't super juicy, but larger tomatoes will be fine as long as you seed them first and drain off some juice before cooking. The final dish wants to be saucy but not soupy.

As for the fish, you can keep it in one large fillet or cut it into portions before cooking, but aim for uniform thickness. If your fish fillet has a thin end, simply fold it under so it matches the thicker end.

SERVES 2 OR 3

1 pound (450 g) cherry tomatoes, halved (go for a mix of colors and shapes), or larger tomatoes, seeded and cut into chunks

Kosher salt

Kernels from 1 ear corn

¼ cup (30 g) roughly chopped pitted olives, such as Castelvetrano or Kalamata (optional)

1 tablespoon drained capers

1 ounce (30 g) sliced salami, preferably fennel salami, cut into thin strips (optional)

2 garlic cloves, very finely chopped

Freshly ground black pepper

1 teaspoon roughly chopped fresh rosemary or thyme

A few leaves of fresh basil, torn or sliced

½ teaspoon finely grated lemon zest

¼ teaspoon Aleppo pepper or ⅛ teaspoon chile flakes

¼ cup (60 ml) extra-virgin olive oil

1 pound (450 g) skinless white-fleshed fish fillets, such as cod, ling cod, halibut, or rockfish (don't use a very thin delicate fish such as sole, which would fall apart)

Preheat the oven to 450°F (230°C).

Put the tomatoes in a strainer set over a bowl, toss with 1 teaspoon salt, and let sit for about 20 minutes to drain off some of their juice.

In a large bowl, combine the drained tomatoes, corn, olives (if using), capers, salami (if using), garlic, ½ teaspoon salt, many twists of black pepper, the rosemary, basil, lemon zest, Aleppo pepper, and 3 tablespoons of the olive oil. Toss until all the ingredients are well integrated.

Spread the remaining 1 tablespoon olive oil over the bottom of a 9-by-13-inch (23 by 33 cm) baking dish. Season the fish fillets lightly with salt and pepper and arrange them in a single layer in the dish. Pile the tomato mixture onto the fish.

Roast until the fish is done all the way through (gently pierce it with a knife to separate the flakes and see whether it's opaque in the center), the tomatoes are sizzling and starting to shrivel up a bit, and the juices are thickening and browning around the edges, about 15 minutes. If the fish is done but the tomato mixture hasn't browned or thickened much, you can transfer the fish to a plate, keep warm under foil, and continue cooking the tomatoes until they are ready; note that the tomatoes keep the fish moist, so don't worry too much about overcooking it. It's important to get the tomato mixture bubbling and reduced, rather than just warmed through.

Divide the fish among dinner plates and top with the tomato jumble, spooning the juices over the fish. Serve right away.

Grilled Whole Fish with Tomatoes, Black Olives, and Parsley-Mint Pesto

Summer meals should be fresh, simple, and, preferably, cooked and eaten outdoors. This dish is all that and more, needing not much accompaniment other than some nice bread, which you could grill alongside the fish. The pesto takes only minutes to make (though I usually have a batch in the fridge anyway), so prep for this dish is minimal.

I love grilling whole fish, for the look and for the yummy bits of flesh that cling to the bones, but if you're not a look-'em-in-the-eye type of fish eater, by all means use fillets or steaks for this; swordfish steaks would be brilliant. For fillets, either spread the pesto and lemon on one side and don't flip the fish, or cook one side first, flip, and then add the pesto and lemon. (Pictured on page 166)

SERVES 2

Parsley-Mint Pesto with Walnuts (recipe follows) or other good pesto

2 small whole fish, such as trout or branzino, about 1 pound (450 g) each, cleaned

Enough thin lemon slices to line the inside of the fish

Extra-virgin olive oil

Kosher salt and freshly ground black pepper

About 2 cups (450 g) fresh tomato chunks or a mix of chunks and halved cherry tomatoes (you could also use Blasted Cherry Tomatoes, page 151, or Cherry Tomato Confit, page 231)

½ cup (90 g) pitted Kalamata or other good-quality olives

Pinch of Aleppo pepper or chile flakes

Heat a grill to medium-high.

Spread a thin layer of the pesto on the inside of each fish and then arrange a layer of lemon slices on the pesto. Rub the exterior of the fish with olive oil and season with salt and black pepper.

Grill the fish until it's cooked through, flipping once during cooking. The rule of thumb is 10 minutes of cooking time for each 1 inch (2.5 cm) of thickness, so a 1-pound (450 g) trout would probably take a total of 8 to 10 minutes.

While the fish is grilling, toss the tomatoes with the olives and season generously with salt, black pepper, Aleppo pepper, and a drizzle of olive oil. Taste and adjust the seasoning until the topping is zesty and delicious.

Put the grilled fish on a platter or plates, drizzle or spread with a generous amount of the remaining pesto, tumble on the tomato-olive mixture, and serve right away, passing any extra pesto at the table.

PARSLEY-MINT PESTO WITH WALNUTS

MAKES ABOUT 1 CUP (240 G)

2 cups (60 g) lightly packed fresh flat-leaf parsley leaves and tender stems

1 cup (30 g) lightly packed fresh mint leaves

½ cup (55 g) chopped walnuts

1 small garlic clove

1 teaspoon finely grated lemon zest

Kosher salt

½ cup (120 ml) walnut oil or extra-virgin olive oil or a mix

In a food processor, combine the parsley, mint, walnuts, garlic, lemon zest, and ¼ teaspoon salt and pulse a few times to make a rough puree. With the machine running, drizzle in the oil, stopping when all the oil is blended, in order to keep a slightly chunky texture. Or, if you'd prefer a smoother pesto, keep processing. Store in the refrigerator for up to 3 days.

Tomatoes, Shrimp, and Chickpeas Baked with Feta and Crunchy Crumbs

Who doesn't love a casserole, especially one that's built around tangy tomatoes and creamy chickpeas, with a few sweet shrimp tucked beneath a layer of crunchy bread crumbs?

The dish is ideal for serving to guests, as you can prepare the tomatoes and chickpeas up to a few hours ahead, then add the shrimp, feta, and crumbs and bake once your friends have arrived. The consistency is fairly saucy, so serve this with a bowl of plain basmati rice or polenta; bread is a fine companion as well.

SERVES 4

¼ cup (60 ml) extra-virgin olive oil, plus 1 tablespoon for the bread crumbs

1 cup (150 g) finely chopped onion

Kosher salt

3 or 4 garlic cloves, very finely chopped

1½ teaspoons sweet or hot smoked paprika

1 teaspoon ground cumin

¼ teaspoon chile flakes, plus more to taste

One 28-ounce (794 g) can whole peeled tomatoes and the juices

One 15-ounce (425 g) can chickpeas or cannellini beans, rinsed and drained (or 1½ cups cooked-from-scratch beans)

2 teaspoons finely grated lemon zest, plus more to taste

3 tablespoons fresh lemon juice, plus more to taste

Freshly ground black pepper

NOTE

If you're shellfish-averse, you could substitute some chunks of halibut or cod and/or some thick slices of Spanish chorizo sausage . . . or skip the meats and keep things vegetarian.

In a large skillet, heat ¼ cup (60 ml) of the olive oil over medium-high heat. Add the onion and ½ teaspoon salt and cook, stirring, until the onion is looking juicy, 4 to 5 minutes. Add the garlic and keep cooking until everything is soft and fragrant, another minute or so. Don't let the onion or garlic brown; reduce the heat if you need to. Stir in the smoked paprika, cumin, and chile flakes and cook for another few seconds to bloom the spices.

Add the tomatoes, ripping each one into a few pieces as you add them. Pay attention to the stem ends of the tomatoes, which can be dense and hard and if so, should be discarded. Pour in the tomato juices.

Add the drained chickpeas, lemon zest, and lemon juice and season the mixture with a bit more salt and a few twists of black pepper.

Bring the mixture to a simmer and cook, stirring now and then, until the consistency has thickened and the flavors have blended, 10 to 15 minutes. I like to smash some of the chickpeas with a wooden spoon during cooking, which will bind the ingredients and make the mixture feel more integrated.

Fold in the fresh herbs. Taste and adjust the seasoning, adding more salt, black pepper, chile flakes, lemon zest, and/or lemon juice until everything is lovely and bright. Remove from the heat.

continues

continues

About ⅓ cup (10 g) chopped fresh tender herbs (choose one or more from dill, cilantro, mint, or parsley)

1 pound (450 g) shrimp (any size), preferably wild, peeled and deveined

4 ounces (115 g) feta cheese, preferably Valbreso, a creamy French sheep's-milk cheese, crumbled

½ cup (25 g) coarse bread crumbs, homemade or panko-style

Preheat the oven to 400°F (200°C).

If your skillet is ovenproof, keep the mixture where it is. If not, transfer the mixture to a baking dish. Nestle the shrimp into the tomato mixture, trying to cover them so they don't overcook in the oven.

Distribute the feta over the top. In a small bowl, stir together the bread crumbs and the remaining 1 tablespoon oil and sprinkle them in an even layer over the top.

Transfer to the oven and bake until the juices are bubbling around the edges of the dish and the shrimp are fully cooked, 15 to 20 minutes. If you have shrimp larger than 13/20 per pound (450 g), you might need another couple of minutes in order to get them fully cooked.

Let the dish rest for about 5 minutes so the juices can thicken, then serve it up.

Roast Chicken Thighs with Sheet-Pan Tomato-Onion Compote

This is one of those amazing sheet-pan suppers, a dish that requires no precision or fussing and yet delivers an attractive, delicious main dish that needs only a salad or some boiled new potatoes as accompaniment. Tomatoes and onion are a constant in the dish, but all the other players can be switched up according to the offerings at the market or garden, such as plums, which add a sweetness that pairs beautifully with the thyme, and any number of chiles or sweet peppers (see the ideas below).

Though this is an unfussy recipe, every batch of tomatoes will be different, so pay attention as they are roasting and giving off juice. You want all your chicken pieces to brown and the other ingredients to caramelize a bit and give off juices, but you don't want the juices to burn nor other bits to blacken. Check a couple of times during cooking and stir things up if they are not behaving.

SERVES 3 OR 4

2 pounds (900 g) cherry tomatoes or other smallish tomatoes, halved, or larger tomatoes, cut into chunks

1 large onion (12 ounces/340 g), cut into ¼-inch (6 mm) slices

6 to 8 garlic cloves, crushed

¼ cup (60 ml) extra-virgin olive oil, plus more for drizzling

¼ teaspoon Aleppo pepper or chile flakes, plus more to taste

2 tablespoons roughly chopped fresh thyme, marjoram, or rosemary

Kosher salt

2¼ pounds (1 kg) bone-in, skin-on chicken thighs (about 6 medium)

Freshly ground black pepper

2 tablespoons (30 g) cold butter (optional)

Preheat the oven to 450°F (230°C).

In a large bowl, combine the tomatoes, onion, garlic, olive oil, Aleppo pepper, herbs, and 1 teaspoon salt and toss until everything's nicely mixed.

Season the chicken thighs generously on both sides with salt and pepper. Drizzle the chicken thighs with a little bit of olive oil and arrange them on a large sheet pan, with space between the pieces. Distribute the tomato mixture and any juices around the chicken in an even layer, without covering the chicken.

Roast until the chicken is totally tender when pierced with a knife and the internal temperature reads 175°F/79°C on an instant-read thermometer, 35 to 45 minutes. (Note that you need to cook the chicken only to 165°F/74°C for safety, but I like cooking dark meat longer for the most succulent, tender texture.) During roasting, check that the tomato mixture isn't burning. You want the vegetables to release juices, collapse, and brown slightly, but you don't want them to burn onto the pan. If they're getting too dark, pour in a few spoonfuls of water or chicken broth, or if the tomatoes are spaced far apart, scooch them closer together for protection from the intense heat.

Transfer the chicken to a serving platter and keep warm. Put a large sieve or colander over a bowl and carefully scrape the tomato mixture into the sieve. Make sure you catch all the juices. If there are browned (but not burnt) juices on the pan, deglaze them by pouring on a little bit of water and scraping to dissolve. Add this liquid to the vegetable juices in

the bowl. Give the juices a taste, and if they don't taste like an intense sauce, simmer in a small saucepan for a few minutes to reduce and concentrate the flavors. Taste and adjust with more salt, black pepper, and/or Aleppo pepper as needed. Whisk in the butter, if using.

After the tomato "compote" has drained for a few minutes, arrange it on the chicken platter as an accompaniment. Serve right away, passing a pitcher of the reserved juices at the table to drizzle over the chicken and tomatoes.

Or Try These Ideas

PLUMS AND SHALLOTS: Reduce the tomatoes to 1 pound (450 g) and add ½ pound (225 g) plums, pitted and cut into wedges. Use ¾ pound (340 g) shallots instead of the onion.

GREEN BEANS AND RED PEPPERS: Add about ½ pound (225 g) trimmed green beans and 1 or 2 red bell peppers, cut into ½-inch (1.25 cm) slices, to the tomato mixture. Increase the olive oil a bit to make sure the vegetables are well coated.

POTATO AND LEEK: Use 1 large leek, white and light green parts, cut into ½-inch (1.25 cm) slices instead of the onion. Add about 1 pound (450 g) Yukon Gold potatoes, cut into 1-inch (2.5 cm) chunks (peel them only if the skin looks tough), to the tomato mixture.

Chicken Schnitzel with Tomato and Fennel Salad

Schnitzel is often served with mashed potatoes and peas, which are delicious but mellow, so try it with a tomato salad as a bright contrast to the rich fried chicken. If you can't find fennel or aren't a fan, use celery to get some crunch. Radishes would be nice as well.

SERVES 2

¼ teaspoon Dijon mustard

1 garlic clove, very finely chopped

1 tablespoon fresh lemon juice

Kosher salt and freshly ground black pepper

Extra-virgin olive oil

1 large tomato, cut into small wedges or chunks

⅓ cup (40 g) very finely sliced fennel or celery

2 or 3 radishes, thinly sliced

2 boneless, skinless chicken breasts (about 6 ounces/ 170 g each)

½ cup (65 g) all-purpose flour

1 egg, beaten

1 cup (50 g) panko bread crumbs

1 tablespoon (15 g) butter, plus more as needed

¼ cup (45 g) pitted Kalamata or other nice olives (optional)

¼ cup (7 g) lightly packed roughly chopped fresh mint, basil, flat-leaf parsley, and/or dill

In a small bowl, whisk together the mustard, garlic, and lemon juice and season generously with salt and pepper. Taste to see that the seasoning is zippy enough, then whisk in 3 tablespoons olive oil.

In a large bowl, toss the dressing with the tomato, fennel, and radishes. Set aside.

If the chicken breasts are already quite thin, just pound them to an even thickness of about ⅜ inch (1 cm). If they're on the thick side or uneven, butterfly them: Place them on the work surface and, with your knife parallel to the surface, cut them almost in half but not all the way through, so you can open them like a book. Then pound out any uneven spots so the whole thing is about ⅜ inch (1 cm) thick.

Get set up for coating the chicken, because this can be messy if you're not organized: Put the flour on a plate, the egg in a shallow bowl or plate, and the panko on another plate. Season both sides of a chicken cutlet with salt and pepper, then dredge in the flour, shaking off excess, then in the egg, and then right into the panko, patting to make an even coating. Repeat with the other cutlet. Set up a plate lined with paper towels for draining the fried chicken and get your plates—and dining partner—ready, because you want to serve schnitzel directly from the skillet.

Heat a very large skillet over medium-high heat. Add 2 tablespoons olive oil and the butter. When the butter stops foaming, add the chicken. (If your skillet isn't large enough to hold both cutlets comfortably, cook them separately and keep the first one warm in a low oven, adding more oil and butter to the skillet as needed.) Cook the cutlets until the crust gets nicely browned on the first side, about 3 minutes, then carefully flip and cook the other side. If the cutlets are thin, they will cook quickly, so be careful not to overcook them.

Drain the cutlets for a few seconds on the paper towels, then transfer to dinner plates. Add the olives (if using) and herbs to the bowl of tomatoes. Place a pile of salad on top of each cutlet. Serve immediately.

French Chicken Fricassee with Vinegar and Tomatoes

I learned to make this dish when I was at La Varenne cooking school in Paris about a hundred years ago, and I still make it often. The vinegar interacts with the tomatoes as both ingredients reduce to create a deeply savory but bright sauce.

Yes, you can use chicken breasts if you prefer, but use bone-in, skin-on in order to keep the chicken moist. As with so many braised dishes, the leftovers are delicious tossed with pasta or as a topping for polenta. Just pick the chicken from the bones, combine with the sauce that you've loosened with a bit more broth or water, and fold together with some cooked penne or ladle over creamy polenta.

SERVES 4

4 bone-in, skin-on chicken thighs plus 4 drumsticks, or 4 chicken leg quarters (about 2 pounds/900 g total)

Kosher salt and freshly ground black pepper

Extra-virgin olive oil

2 ounces (60 g) pancetta, finely chopped

½ cup (75 g) finely chopped onion

½ cup (65 g) finely chopped carrot

½ cup (65 g) finely chopped celery

½ cup (65 g) finely chopped fennel (optional)

4 or 5 garlic cloves, finely chopped

Chile flakes

½ cup (120 ml) sherry vinegar or good red wine vinegar of your choice (balsamic also works nicely as long as it's not too sweet)

Trim off and discard any excess skin or fat from the chicken pieces. (Note: If your chicken thighs have a lot of extra skin and fat, which they often do, put the trimmings in a small pan and render out the fat, called schmaltz, and save it, in the refrigerator, to use for frying potatoes.)

Pat the chicken dry with paper towels, then season generously with salt and pepper.

In a heavy skillet that's large enough to hold all the chicken in one comfortable layer, heat a small glug of olive oil over medium-high heat. Add the chicken pieces, skin side down. Reduce the heat to medium, or whatever temperature keeps the chicken quietly sizzling but not crackling or sputtering—you want to take your time with this step to get a nice deep browning without burning. Cook, undisturbed, until the skin is deep golden brown, about 10 minutes. Turn the pieces over and cook for an additional 4 or 5 minutes. Try not to let the pan juices get too dark, as they will add flavor to the dish—if they seem to be heading in that direction, though, reduce the heat.

Transfer the chicken to a plate or tray and pour or spoon off all but about 1 tablespoon of the fat from the pan. (Add it to your potato-frying stash!) Add the pancetta and onion to the pan and cook until the pancetta has rendered its fat and the onion is soft and fragrant, about 5 minutes. Scrape the bottom of the pan as you cook to deglaze (dissolve) any chicken juices.

Add the carrot, celery, fennel (if using), and garlic and season lightly with salt, pepper, and a pinch of chile flakes. Cook until the vegetable mixture—called a mirepoix—starts to soften, about 5 more minutes.

One 14.5-ounce (411 g) can whole peeled tomatoes, drained and chopped

1 cup (240 ml) chicken broth, homemade or low-sodium canned

A few sprigs fresh thyme and/or rosemary

2 tablespoons (30 g) cold butter (optional)

Small handful of chopped fresh flat-leaf parsley, for garnish (optional)

Now, turn on your vent hood fan, stand back from the stove, and pour the vinegar into the skillet. The vinegar probably will produce some sharp fumes, so keep your face away from the pan. Simmer until the vinegar is reduced by almost half, then add the tomatoes, broth, and herb sprigs. Nestle the chicken pieces back into the pan, skin side up.

Cover the pan, adjust the heat to maintain a gentle simmer, and cook until the chicken is cooked all the way through, 30 to 45 minutes, depending on the size of your chicken pieces. For chicken thighs and drumsticks (dark meat), the internal temperature should read about 175°F (79°C) on an instant-read thermometer. (If you decided to use chicken breasts—see headnote—cook only until 165°F/74°C.)

To finish the dish, transfer the chicken to a platter. Spoon off any fat from the surface of the sauce, then increase the heat to medium-high so it bubbles vigorously. Cook just until the sauce has thickened and reduced by about one-third. Retrieve and discard the herb stems.

Take the pan off the heat and stir or swirl in the cold butter, if using, until it has blended into and further thickened (emulsified) the sauce. The butter is optional, but I like the way it softens the edge of the tomato-vinegar. Taste and adjust the seasoning with more salt, pepper, and/or chile flakes.

Pour the sauce over the chicken. Garnish with the chopped parsley, if you like.

Butternut Squash and Apple Cabbage Rolls Baked in Tomato Sauce

My mother never made cabbage rolls, so I have no sentimental attachment to any traditional version, which is usually green cabbage wrapped around a (slightly dense) filling of rice and ground meat, baked in bright red tomato sauce. Comforting, yes, but we can do better!

Try this version, which is much lighter, forgoing the meat in favor of sweet butternut squash and apples with a tangy counterpoint from capers and sun-dried tomatoes. You use a little bit of rice in the filling, and bread crumbs and rich pine nuts provide additional "binding." Cooking the rolls at a high temperature uncovered means the tomato sauce reduces nicely, making it almost like a glaze, and the tops of the rolls become deeply browned.

MAKES 12 ROLLS; SERVES 4 TO 6

Filling

Extra-virgin olive oil

About 3 cups (400 g) ½-inch (1.25 cm) cubes butternut squash

Kosher salt and freshly ground black pepper

1 cup (150 g) finely chopped onion

2 tablespoons finely chopped fresh green chile, such as jalapeño (optional)

1 tablespoon finely chopped fresh ginger or ½ teaspoon ground ginger

3 garlic cloves, very finely chopped

¼ teaspoon chile flakes, plus more to taste

½ cup (100 g) medium- or long-grain white rice

1 large apple (½ pound/225 g), peeled, cored, and cut into ½-inch (1.25 cm) cubes

continues

NOTES

- This dish is a bit time-consuming; however, you can work it into your schedule by making the filling the day ahead—but don't add the rice until you're ready to fill the cabbage leaves. Because all of the hard work can be done ahead, the dish makes a fine centerpiece for an autumn dinner party.

- I prefer Savoy cabbage for its sweet flavor and ease of rolling, but regular green cabbage will work just fine here.

- The leftovers are excellent and can be reheated in a 350°F (180°C) oven until hot all the way through.

MAKE THE FILLING: In a large skillet, heat a generous glug of olive oil over medium-high heat. Add the squash so it's mostly in one layer, season well with salt and pepper, and cook until lightly browned on at least a couple of sides, 7 to 8 minutes. The squash should be close to fully tender at this point. Transfer the squash to a large bowl.

Add a bit more olive oil to the skillet, add the onion, green chile (if using), ginger, garlic, and chile flakes, and continue cooking until the onion is starting to soften, 3 to 4 minutes. Add the rice and apple and cook until the onion and apple are tender and starting to brown a bit around the edges; the rice will still be firm.

Stir in the thyme, then scrape everything into the bowl with the squash. Let the mixture cool slightly and then gently fold in the pine nuts, panko, sun-dried tomatoes, capers (if using), and Parmigiano. Taste and adjust the seasoning with

1 teaspoon chopped fresh thyme

½ cup (65 g) pine nuts (raw or lightly toasted), roughly chopped

½ cup (25 g) panko or other coarse dried bread crumbs

¼ cup (40 g) finely chopped sun-dried tomatoes (either oil-packed or another soft style)

2 tablespoons drained capers, roughly chopped (optional)

½ cup (50 g) finely grated Parmigiano-Reggiano cheese

Cabbage Rolls

1 medium head Savoy cabbage

Kosher salt

Extra-virgin olive oil

½ cup (75 g) chopped onion

One 14.5-ounce (411 g) can whole peeled tomatoes and the juices

1¾ cups (420 ml) chicken or vegetable broth (homemade or low-sodium canned) or Tomato Water (page 70)

2 garlic cloves, smashed

½ cup (50 g) finely grated Parmigiano-Reggiano cheese

Sprigs fresh thyme or rosemary (optional)

more salt, black pepper, and/or chile flakes; you want the filling to be well seasoned.

ASSEMBLE AND BAKE THE CABBAGE ROLLS: With a sturdy paring knife, cut out the core from the cabbage. Peel off any wilted outer leaves, and then proceed to pull off 12 large leaves (or more smaller leaves that you'll piece together to make 12 rolls). Shave off the thick ribs running down the center of the leaves so that the leaves are fully flexible.

Bring a large pot of water to a boil and add about 2 tablespoons salt. Add the cabbage leaves and boil until pliable but not fully cooked; you might want to boil a few at a time. You want them just soft enough to roll without cracking. Drain on paper towels or a clean kitchen towel. (No fabric softener, please!)

Preheat the oven to 425°F (220°C). Choose a baking dish that will hold all the rolls in one layer; a 9-by-13-inch (23 by 33 cm) baking dish works well.

In a medium skillet, heat a glug of olive oil over medium heat. Add the onion, season lightly with salt, and cook until soft but not browned, about 5 minutes. Scatter the onion in an even layer in the baking dish.

Arrange a cabbage leaf on the work surface and spoon about ½ cup of the filling onto the center. Fold the bottom of the leaf over the filling, tucking it in tightly, then fold over the two sides and roll up to make a cylinder. This will be easy and tidy with the large leaves and will get trickier as you piece together smaller leaves, but don't worry; just tuck and fold as necessary to get the filling encased in cabbage. The rolls will stick together better once they're cooked. Arrange the rolls in the baking dish, snugging them to fit tightly in one layer.

Put the tomatoes and their juices in a medium bowl and break them up with your hands. Add the chicken broth and pour the mixture over the cabbage rolls. Tuck the garlic cloves into the dish and top with the Parmigiano. Strew a few herb sprigs over the top, if you like.

Bake the cabbage rolls until they are fully tender and nicely browned on top and the tomato sauce has thickened and browned around the edges, 45 minutes to 1 hour. Let them rest for about 10 minutes so the juices thicken up. Serve with some of the sauce spooned on top. Keep leftovers tightly covered in the fridge for up to 3 days; reheat covered in a 375°F (190°C) oven until the filling is nice and hot.

Tomatoes Stuffed with Spiced Beef Picadillo

As a concept, a stuffed vegetable is brilliant—you can eat the container!—but the reality often falls short of the concept because people undercook the container vegetable in the interest of keeping it intact and tidy. Looks good, but it tastes raw.

For these stuffed tomatoes, I don't care if the tomato collapses a bit, because I know that the slump means it's cooked through and will taste great. The trick is to use tomatoes that are ripe but not super fleshy and wet, such as Early Girl or Black Krim. For a grocery store tomato, try a Campari type; these are smallish tomatoes, so count on 3 per person instead of 2.

SERVES 3 AS A MAIN COURSE, OR 6 AS A SMALL COURSE

6 large firm-ripe tomatoes

Kosher salt

2 tablespoons extra-virgin olive oil, plus more for the tomatoes

¾ cup (110 g) finely chopped onion

3 garlic cloves, finely chopped

1 tablespoon ground cumin

½ teaspoon chipotle powder or hot smoked paprika

⅛ teaspoon ground cinnamon

1 teaspoon chopped fresh thyme or ½ teaspoon dried thyme leaves

1 teaspoon chopped fresh oregano or ½ teaspoon dried oregano leaves

½ pound (225 g) ground beef, preferably grass-fed

⅓ cup (50 g) chopped raisins

½ cup (90 g) finely chopped pimiento-stuffed olives

Freshly ground black pepper

With a sharp knife, cut off the top quarter of each tomato. Discard the stem part and finely chop the flesh; put it in a measuring cup. Scoop out the seeds and pulp from the tomatoes and add that to the chopped tops; measure out about 1 cup (240 ml) and set aside. (Discard the rest or save for making Tomato Water, page 70.) Lightly season the interior of the tomatoes with salt and invert them on a cooling rack set over a sheet pan to catch the drips. If you don't have a rack, just invert them on the sheet pan.

In a large skillet, heat the olive oil over medium heat. Add the onion and cook, stirring, until soft and fragrant, 3 to 4 minutes. Add the garlic and stir for a minute, then stir in 1½ teaspoons salt, the cumin, chipotle powder, cinnamon, thyme, and oregano and cook for about 30 seconds, until very fragrant. Add the beef and cook until most of the pink is gone, about 2 minutes. Add the reserved tomato bits, increase the heat to medium-high, and cook, stirring, until the mixture has slightly thickened and is nicely blended, 5 to 15 minutes, depending on how juicy the tomato pulp is. Think Sloppy Joe consistency. Stir in the raisins and olives. Taste and add more salt if needed.

Preheat the oven to 450°F (230°C).

Rub some olive oil on the outside of the tomatoes and season with salt and pepper. Arrange them in a baking pan and fill them with the beef mixture. Bake until the tomatoes are tender and starting to brown around the shoulders, 30 to 40 minutes. If you see a lot of juices accumulating in the baking dish as you're cooking, spoon them over the tomatoes to moisten the filling and to prevent the juices from burning.

Let the tomatoes rest for about 5 minutes to firm up a bit. For the best flavor, serve warm but not piping hot.

Tender Lamb Meatballs in Tomato Sauce with Fragrant Spices

One of the benefits of a meatball is the way it contributes a ton of flavor and richness to the sauce in which it's cooked. Here I'm using lamb, along with some vaguely Middle Eastern–inspired flavorings, so the tomato sauce becomes fragrant and tangy. The meatballs will be slightly fragile when you brown them, so be gentle; it's a trade-off where slightly hard to handle means a tender final texture.

SERVES 4

¾ cup (40 g) soft fresh bread crumbs

2 tablespoons dry white wine or water

1 pound (450 g) ground lamb

⅓ cup (35 g) finely grated Parmigiano-Reggiano cheese

½ cup (15 g) finely chopped fresh cilantro or mint (or a mix), plus more for garnish

2 tablespoons finely chopped sun-dried tomatoes (oil-packed or another soft type)

5 medium garlic cloves, 2 very finely chopped, 3 smashed

Kosher salt and freshly ground black pepper

Big pinch of Aleppo pepper or chile flakes, plus more as needed

Extra-virgin olive oil

½ cup (75 g) finely chopped onion

1 teaspoon sweet or hot smoked paprika

1 teaspoon ground cumin

½ teaspoon ground allspice

½ teaspoon ground cinnamon

continues

NOTE

These meatballs pair well with many partners: rice, couscous, quinoa, grilled bread, or, of course, pasta or polenta. And they'd be terrific tucked into a pita with fresh greens and a spoonful of yogurt.

In a small bowl, sprinkle the bread crumbs with the wine and toss to moisten them evenly. In a large bowl, with your hands, gently mix the lamb, bread crumbs, Parmigiano, half the chopped cilantro, the sun-dried tomatoes, the chopped garlic, 1 teaspoon salt, many twists of black pepper, and the Aleppo pepper. Don't squeeze or overwork the mixture, but do try to distribute all the ingredients evenly.

Roll the mixture into 16 balls.

In a large skillet, heat a little olive oil (about 2 tablespoons) over medium-high heat. Working in batches to avoid crowding the pan, add a layer of meatballs, leaving enough room between them so you can turn them without breaking, and brown the meatballs gently on all sides. (Because of the cheese, the meatballs may stick a little, so use a spatula to gently dislodge them as you turn them. Take care not to burn the browned bits that stick to the pan; they'll add flavor to the sauce. If they end up burning, scoop them out of the pan.) It should take about 6 minutes per batch.

Transfer the meatballs to a plate, pour off any fat from the pan, and add another pour of olive oil. Add the onion, smoked paprika, cumin, allspice, and cinnamon. Cook over medium-high heat, stirring almost constantly, scraping up any browned bits from the meatballs, until the onion is very soft and starting to brown lightly and the spices are fragrant, 3 to 4 minutes. Add the smashed garlic and cook for another minute or so.

Add the broth, all the tomatoes, about ⅓ cup (80 ml) of the juice from the tomatoes (discard or freeze the rest of the

1 cup (240 ml) chicken broth, homemade or low-sodium canned

One 14.5-ounce (411 g) can whole peeled tomatoes, drained and juices reserved

1 tablespoon pomegranate molasses or 1 teaspoon balsamic vinegar

Cooked grain or pasta, for serving (see Note)

¼ cup (60 g) plain yogurt

juice for later), and the remaining chopped cilantro. Crush the tomatoes with a wooden spoon or a spatula until they're in small pieces.

Nestle the meatballs in the sauce, cover the pan, and adjust the heat to a lively simmer. Cook the meatballs until they're no longer pink inside, shaking the pan so the meatballs get evenly moistened and heated, 5 to 10 minutes.

Transfer the meatballs to a clean plate, increase the heat to high, and boil the sauce until it's fairly thick, glossy, and very tasty, about 5 minutes. Stir in the pomegranate molasses. Taste and adjust the seasoning with more salt, black pepper, and Aleppo pepper if necessary.

Return the meatballs to the sauce and gently reheat them. Serve immediately over your choice of a base (grain or pasta), with a spoonful of yogurt drizzled over each serving and a shower of chopped herbs.

SUN-DRIED TOMATOES

I've been cooking long enough to remember when a sun-dried tomato was an exotic ingredient whose use would signal "gourmet cook." The chewy-but-tender, sweet-tart semi-dried tomatoes were a revelation to me when I first started on my cooking journey— so Mediterranean!—and I happily added them to salads, pastas, dressings, stuffings, and more.

I use them in my cooking today, but with restraint. It's difficult to find brands that have the same bright flavor and succulent texture as in the past, or at least my memory of the past. Over the decades, as their popularity grew and production quantities increased, the quality of commercial sun-dried tomatoes diminished. Mass-produced sun-dried tomatoes are no longer made from perfectly ripe tomatoes slowly dried in the sun, but are rather run-of-the-mill fruit dehydrated in a factory somewhere, leathery rather than fleshy and slightly bitter rather than sweet.

Nonetheless, good quality sun-dried tomatoes are available from Italian import stores as well as in many grocery stores. You'll find three forms:

1. Completely dried, similar to a dried mushroom. I don't use these, as I can't be bothered with rehydrating.

2. Chewy-tender in a bag, much like dried apricots. These are easy to use and don't contribute any oil or seasonings to your dish, which can be a good thing.

3. Jarred in olive oil, often with other seasonings. These tend to be the most succulent, though the oiliness can make chopping a bit sloppy.

Use sun-dried tomatoes as you would any dried fruit—cut into small bits and added to a dish for a pop of sweet-tart flavor.

As for homemade dried tomatoes, I have tried several methods over the years using a home dehydrator but never loved the results. Getting the tomatoes dry enough to be safe from spoilage meant they were hard and leathery, and the flavor nuances were lost. I'll keep experimenting.

Braised Beef Short Ribs with Tomato, Dried Porcini, and Red Wine

In this dish, tomato shows a different side of its personality. Unlike the sunny, fruity flavors that we enjoy in so many tomato dishes, here we see tomato's darker side, a deep savoriness that develops after long cooking with the dried porcini and well-browned short ribs. Among fruits and vegetables, tomatoes contain one of the highest levels of the umami-producing compounds called glutamates, and when they work in concert with the inosinic acid found in meat and the guanylates in the dried mushrooms, two more umami sources, the result is nirvana for umami freaks. (See page 10.)

I love this dish with polenta, a perfect foil for the rich gravy, but boiled potatoes, wide egg noodles, or spaetzle would be excellent as well.

SERVES 4 WITH LEFTOVERS

2½ pounds (1.1 kg) beef short ribs

Kosher salt

½ ounce (15 g) dried porcini

Extra-virgin olive oil

One 750 ml bottle dry fruity red wine that's not too tannic, such as a Beaujolais or light Rhône

About 2 cups (250 g) finely chopped onion

About ¾ cup (100 g) finely diced carrot

About ¾ cup (100 g) finely diced celery

4 or 5 garlic cloves, smashed

2 tablespoons tomato paste

One 28-ounce (794 g) can whole peeled tomatoes with the juices, broken up with your hands

A big sprig fresh rosemary

1 bay leaf

continues

Up to 1 hour before you will start working, season the short ribs with 1 tablespoon salt and let sit on the counter so the meat can get closer to room temperature.

In a small bowl, soak the porcini until they're soft in enough warm water to easily cover them, at least 30 minutes.

In a large heavy pot or Dutch oven, heat a glug of olive oil over medium-high heat. Blot any moisture from the short ribs and brown them on all sides, taking your time so that you get nice caramelization. This could take up to 30 minutes to get all the ribs nicely browned. Take care not to burn the juices that are forming in the bottom of the pan, as they will be the basis of your sauce; lower the temperature if needed. If a lot of fat is accumulating in the pan, spoon it off.

Remove the short ribs and set aside. Pour off any remaining fat, then add a big splash of the wine to deglaze those nice juices, scraping with a silicone spatula to dissolve them all. Pour the pan juices into a bowl and set aside.

Rinse and dry the pot, then add more olive oil, and then the onion, carrot, celery, and a pinch of salt. Cook over medium heat until the vegetables are soft and fragrant, about 5 minutes.

Add the garlic and cook for another minute or two. Increase the heat a bit, add the tomato paste, and cook, stirring and scraping, to brown the paste and to brown the vegetables just a touch (watch out that you don't burn the garlic).

Meanwhile, drain and chop the porcini and set aside.

Add about 1 cup (240 ml) of the wine to the pot with the vegetables and cook over medium-high heat until the wine has reduced to a glaze, about 5 minutes.

continues

1 dried red chile, such as cayenne or chile de árbol (optional)

Freshly ground black pepper

Pinch of sugar, if needed

¼ cup (7 g) chopped fresh flat-leaf parsley

Polenta, potatoes, or noodles, for serving

Add the beef to the pot, along with the canned tomatoes and their juices, the remaining wine, the reserved pan juices, the chopped porcini, the rosemary, bay leaf, dried chile (if using), 2 teaspoons salt, and many twists of black pepper. Adjust the heat so that when the pot is covered, the liquid simmers merrily but isn't actually boiling, which would toughen the meat.

Cook, turning the short ribs once or twice, until the meat is extremely tender, which could take from 1½ hours to more than 3 hours; it just depends on your meat and the thickness and character of that cut. It's likely that the flat rib bones will slide out of the meat, which is fine.

When the short ribs are very tender, transfer them to a big plate or platter, tent with foil, and let rest for a good 15 minutes.

Meanwhile, to finish the sauce, spoon off any visible fat and discard it. (Note: If you make this a day ahead, refrigerate the sauce separately from the meat. The fat will harden on top of the sauce, making it very easy to degrease.)

Scoop out all but 1 cup (240 ml) or so of the sauce and strain it through a fine-mesh sieve back into the pot, pushing on the solids to extract all the flavor and a bit of the cooked vegetables, which will give the sauce texture. (You can strain all of the sauce for a smoother consistency, if you like, or don't strain any and leave it slightly chunky with vegetables.)

Taste the sauce. You'll probably want to simmer it a bit to concentrate the flavor and the consistency so that it cloaks the meat nicely. Once it's reduced to your liking, adjust the flavor with more salt and/or pepper. If it's a bit sharp, stir in a pinch of sugar.

Arrange the short ribs on plates or a platter and cover with plenty of sauce. Shower with the parsley. Serve with the accompaniment of your choice, and pass the rest of the sauce at the table.

TOMATO PASTE (CONSERVA)

It's easy to understand why you might not think to make your own tomato paste. After all, most recipes call for only a small amount. Would homemade-quality even be perceived? And worth the effort? After making my own tomato paste for the last few years, I can answer "yes" and "yes" to both those questions. Homemade tomato paste, called *conserva* by Italians, does indeed taste better than store-bought, and, because it's easy to make, it's definitely worth the small amount of effort, though my one caveat is that you need a lot of tomatoes, so it could get expensive if you don't grow your own.

But when you have plentiful garden tomatoes for free (free, that is, if you don't count the mulch, the compost, the tomato seeds and starts, the fish emulsion, the stakes and twine, the new garden gloves, that cute harvesting basket . . .), you can make a year's supply of tomato paste in an afternoon, and even customize a few batches by making a "single-varietal" tomato paste or flavoring a batch with garlic or herbs.

Managing the Variables

Choose the most flavorful tomato, even if it's not a "paste" type. Ironically, I never make tomato paste with paste tomatoes, such as a Roma type. I use whatever tomatoes I have in abundance. Any ripe tomato with delicious flavor will work fine; a more watery variety will just take longer to reduce to a paste.

Start the batch on the stove to get the juices flowing and break down the flesh a bit, then blend in a blender and strain. I don't always strain out the seeds and skin, as I don't mind a bit of texture, and I am a fairly lazy cook. Some people cook the puree on the stovetop to thicken before transferring it to the oven, but that does require some attention, and the simmering puree tends to erupt like lava from time to time. And some cooks use a higher oven temperature to speed up the process. Low and slow works for me, but as you get comfortable with making tomato paste, you'll fine-tune your process.

Do pay attention as the paste is cooking, especially toward the end of the process, as you don't want the paste around the edge of the pan to darken too much, which would make it bitter. But there's no real harm in opening the oven door a million times to check on the progress of the paste because you're cooking these low and slow anyway, so losing a few degrees of oven heat won't have any adverse effects.

Some people put their paste in canning jars and process them like canned tomatoes, but I like to put my tomato paste into small vacuum-seal food-saver bags and freeze them. You can either just break off a portion of the frozen paste and drop it in your soup pot or other dish, or quickly thaw the paste in warm water. To save any unused tomato paste, fold over the edge of the food-saver bag and secure with a binder clip and pop into the refrigerator.

TOMATO PASTE (CONSERVA)

MAKES ABOUT 1 POUND (450 G)

About 10 pounds (4.5 kg) tomatoes, cored, any blemishes removed, and cut into chunks if large

1 tablespoon kosher salt

Optional flavorings of your choice: leaves or sprigs of basil and/or flat-leaf parsley, whole peeled garlic cloves, chile flakes

Extra-virgin olive oil

Put the tomatoes into one or two big pots and add the salt and any optional flavorings. Bring to a gentle simmer over medium heat. Cook, stirring frequently, until the tomatoes are starting to break down and get saucy, about 25 minutes. Let cool to a temperature that won't burn you if the sauce splashes.

Working in batches, puree the tomato sauce in a blender and pass through a not-too-fine sieve into a large bowl. If you have a large food mill, you can go straight from the pot to the mill set over a bowl. If you've added herbs on stems, be sure to fish them out before pureeing so they don't add a strong "stemmy" flavor.

Preheat the oven to 275°F (130°C). Pour the tomato puree into two baking dishes, such as 9-by-13-inch (23 by 33 cm) Pyrex. Place the dishes in the oven and cook, stirring and scraping the tomato from the edges into the center about every hour. Watch that the edges aren't actually blackening, which would make the paste bitter. As the tomato puree reduces, the risk of darkening and burning increases, so pay attention. Once the volume has reduced by half, combine the two amounts in one dish and continue to cook until the paste is thick, deep crimson, and very delicious and sweet, 4 to 6 hours.

Let the finished paste cool, transfer to a fresh container, cover with a thin layer of olive oil, and store in the fridge for up to 3 weeks. Or portion into smaller containers and freeze. (A vacuum-type food-saver system works brilliantly with tomato paste.) Or preserve in canning jars using a boiling-water bath (follow the instructions in a good canning reference; see Resources, page 239).

Good Things to Do with Conserva

Use anywhere your recipe calls for tomato paste, but homemade is so good, you can use it as a sandwich spread or pizza topping, on grilled flatbread, or swirled into a pot of cooked beans.

Tomato
Side Dishes

Provençale Tomatoes

I went to France for the first time right after college. I learned to conjugate French verbs from my teachers at the Sorbonne, and I learned to make tomates à la provençale from my French boyfriend.

The bread crumbs are the key here—use lots of them, and make them from scratch so they are big and irregular and will keep some crispness even as they drink up the tangy tomato juices. These tomatoes are excellent served with steak and some boiled new potatoes.

SERVES 4

1½ cups (75 g) coarse fresh bread crumbs

½ cup (15 g) roughly chopped fresh flat-leaf parsley

½ cup (50 g) finely grated Parmigiano-Reggiano cheese

1 or 2 garlic cloves, very finely chopped

1 teaspoon finely grated lemon zest

Extra-virgin olive oil

Kosher salt and freshly ground black pepper

4 large firm-ripe tomatoes, cored

Preheat the oven to 425°F (220°C).

In a medium bowl, toss together the bread crumbs, parsley, Parmigiano, garlic, lemon zest, about 3 tablespoons olive oil, ½ teaspoon kosher salt, and several twists of black pepper.

Cut the tomatoes into very thick slices, about ¾ inch (2 cm) if the tomato allows it. If you end up with some thinner end slices, stack them up. If you can, gently squeeze out the seeds; you don't want the tomatoes to be super wet.

Lightly oil a baking dish, arrange the tomato slices in the dish, and top with the crumbs—you will have a lot! It's okay if some fall off the tomatoes into the dish. Lay a sheet of foil over everything, keeping it very loose; this is just to protect the crumbs from browning too fast, but you want the liquid from the tomatoes to be able to evaporate, so don't seal the foil against the dish.

Bake for 10 minutes, then remove the foil and continue cooking until the tomatoes have softened, their juices are bubbling around the edges, and the crumbs are golden brown, another 10 minutes or so.

Let the tomatoes rest out of the oven for about 10 minutes before scooping up to serve.

Or Try This Idea

Put a half anchovy fillet on each tomato slice before topping with the crumbs.

Long-Cooked Romano Beans with Tomatoes and Savory

Romano beans are flat, long, slightly pale green beans that look a bit like snow peas gone wild. Romanos truly need long cooking; otherwise, they're tough. If you can't find them, just use regular green beans, but opt for mature, larger ones rather than delicate haricots verts. Those are best just steamed and anointed with a tiny bit of butter and salt.

If you're used to your green beans being cooked only until "crisp-tender," this dish may be a revelation. The grassy green flavor of barely cooked beans will give way to a deep sweetness and silky texture that can only come with long, slow cooking . . . in a lot of olive oil. The dish gets its tension from sweetly acidic tomatoes and a hint of a resinous herb such as savory, marjoram, or rosemary. I love to include the dish as part of an antipasto spread, as the flavor and texture of the beans are best at room temperature. As simple as this dish is, it always gets raves from guests.

SERVES 4

Extra-virgin olive oil

1 bunch scallions, roots and top 1 inch (2.5 cm) of greens trimmed off, cut into ½-inch (1.25 cm) pieces

2 or 3 garlic cloves, roughly chopped

¼ teaspoon chile flakes, plus more to taste

1½ pounds (680 g) Romano beans, stem ends snipped or broken off

1 pound (450 g) juicy tomatoes, cut into large chunks

½ cup (120 ml) chicken broth, homemade or low-sodium canned, or water

A big sprig fresh summer or winter savory, marjoram, or rosemary

Kosher salt and freshly ground black pepper

Fresh lemon juice or sherry vinegar

In a large skillet (big enough to hold all the beans and tomatoes), heat about ¼ cup (60 ml) olive oil (a bit more is fine) over medium-high heat. Add the scallions, garlic, and chile flakes and cook until the scallions are softening, about 1 minute; don't let the garlic brown at all.

Add the beans and sauté for a few minutes to coat with oil and get the party started. Add the tomatoes, broth, and herb sprig and season generously with salt and pepper.

Adjust the heat so that the beans simmer gently when covered. Cover with a lid (or foil) and cook until the beans are quite tender (take a bite), the tomatoes have broken down, and the juices look saucy, about 30 minutes, stirring once or twice along the way.

Uncover the skillet, increase the heat a bit, and cook until the tomatoes get jammy and coat the beans nicely, another 3 to 5 minutes.

Finish with a squeeze of lemon juice or a few drops of sherry vinegar. Taste and adjust with more lemon, salt, pepper, and/or chile flakes. Serve the beans slightly warm or at room temperature. They will keep in the fridge for 3 days; reheat in a saucepan or the microwave.

Or Try This Idea

Instead of fresh tomatoes, use any of the roasted or confited tomatoes:
Classic Roasted Tomatoes (page 48), Low and Slow Roasted Plum
Tomatoes (page 165), Blasted Cherry Tomatoes (page 151), Roasted
Canned Tomatoes (page 235), or Cherry Tomato Confit (page 231).
To use any of these preserved tomatoes rather than fresh ones,
add them to the pan after the beans have been cooking for about
15 minutes. You'll probably want to cut plum tomato halves into
quarters or chunks.

Tomato, Potato, and Gruyère Gratin

Creamy potatoes and bright tomatoes pair splendidly flavorwise, but cooking the two together can be challenging. The acid in the tomatoes prevents the cellulose in the potatoes (and any vegetables and dried beans) from softening properly, so to sidestep that problem, parcook the potatoes before assembling the gratin—it's an added step, yes, but it's easy enough to do and makes all the difference.

SERVES 4

4 tablespoons (60 g) butter, melted

1 tablespoon Dijon mustard

1 tablespoon chopped fresh thyme or 1 teaspoon dried thyme

1½ pounds (680 g) Yukon Gold or other medium-starch potato, peeled and sliced ⅛ inch (3 mm) thick

Kosher salt

1½ pounds (680 g) tomatoes, sliced ¼ inch (6 mm) thick

Freshly ground black pepper

1½ cups (180 g) grated Gruyère or Comté cheese

In a large bowl, whisk together the melted butter, mustard, and thyme; set aside.

In a large saucepan or deep skillet, combine the potatoes with water to cover by about 1 inch (2.5 cm) and add 1 tablespoon salt. Bring to a simmer and cook until the potatoes are just barely tender, about 5 minutes; be sure to cook gently so the slices don't break up.

Gently drain the potato slices and transfer to the bowl with the butter-mustard mixture. Carefully fold to coat all the slices; your hands are probably the best tool for this.

Preheat the oven to 375°F (190°C).

In a 9-by-13-inch (23 by 33 cm) baking dish, arrange a layer of tomato slices, using about half the slices, and season with salt and pepper. Arrange a layer of potatoes over the tomatoes, again using about half the slices; season with salt and pepper. Distribute about half the cheese over the potatoes. Repeat with the remaining ingredients: tomatoes, potatoes, cheese.

Bake until the potatoes are fully tender, the cheese is browned on top, and all the juices are bubbling, 1 hour to 1 hour 20 minutes. Let the gratin rest for 5 minutes before serving.

Paella-Style Tomato-Saffron Rice

All elements of paella are wonderful, but the tomatoey rice is the thing that makes it so moreish, so here you use the same method to create rice that's infused with flavor, tender but not mushy, and—if all goes well—with a golden crunchy layer on the bottom, called a *socarrat* in Spanish. If you're not a saffron fan, you can skip it and the rice will still be delicious. Serve this with grilled vegetables and some grilled shrimp or chicken for an easy deconstructed paella.

SERVES 3 OR 4

1¾ cups (420 ml) chicken or vegetable broth, homemade or low-sodium canned, or more if needed

1¾ cups (420 ml) Tomato Water (page 70) or another 1¾ cups (420 ml) broth

Pinch of saffron threads

Kosher salt

Extra-virgin olive oil

½ medium onion, grated

1 large tomato, grated

2 garlic cloves, very finely chopped

1 teaspoon sweet or hot smoked paprika

Freshly ground black pepper

1 cup (200 g) medium-grain paella rice, preferably a Spanish rice such as bomba

¼ cup (7 g) chopped fresh flat-leaf parsley (optional)

2 or 3 small lemon wedges (optional)

NOTE

If it's easier, instead of grating the onion and tomato, pulse them in a food processor. Just be sure not to process all the way to a puree.

In a saucepan, combine the broth, tomato water, saffron, and 1 teaspoon salt and bring to just below a simmer. Keep warm, but don't let the liquid simmer, or it will reduce, and your ratio of water to rice will be off.

In a 10- to 11-inch (25 to 28 cm) heavy-bottomed skillet, heat a glug of olive oil over medium-high heat. Add the onion and cook, stirring, just until it softens, 3 to 4 minutes.

Add the tomato, garlic, paprika, 1 teaspoon salt, and many twists of black pepper. Cook over brisk heat, stirring and scraping with a flat wooden spoon or spatula, until the tomato has rendered its liquid and the mixture is getting thick and turning darker, 5 to 7 minutes.

Add the rice and cook, stirring, for about 1 minute so the rice toasts and is coated by the tomato mixture. Add ½ cup (120 ml) of the broth, stirring to blend. Adjust the heat and simmer gently until most of the liquid has been absorbed, about 5 minutes. Add another ½ cup (120 ml) and continue like this until all the liquid has been added and the rice is not quite tender—take a bite, and look for a pinpoint of white in the center. After the first 3 or 4 additions of liquid, stop stirring and cook the rice undisturbed, which should help the crust on the bottom to form. If you've used all the liquid and the rice seems far from tender, add more liquid, ¼ cup (60 ml) at a time. The whole process should take about 25 minutes.

Cover the pan with a lid or foil and cook for another minute or two, until the rice is completely tender. Remove the lid, increase the heat to medium-high, and cook for another 1 to 2 minutes to encourage a crust to form on the bottom. You won't always get a good crust, but any crunchy bits will add depth and texture.

Remove the pan from the heat and let the rice sit for a couple of minutes before either serving it from the skillet or scraping it up and piling into a serving bowl. Top with the parsley and serve with lemon wedges (if using).

Susie's Tomato and Zucchini Gratin

Susie Middleton and I became great friends when we worked together at *Fine Cooking* magazine many moons ago. She developed countless fantastic recipes, but this one is my favorite. Over the years, I have modified it in a million ways, to suit the vegetables I have, to align with the rest of the menu, or to match my whim of the day. This is one of the best things about the dish—it is flexible and cooperative, as long as you do one thing: Cook it long enough!

As the vegetables cook, they release a lot of juice. You need to cook the dish until the juices reduce, concentrate, and begin to brown and bubble around the edges of the vegetables, which will look noticeably shriveled. So many good things in cooking happen in the final minutes, when the sugars and proteins cross a threshold from merely "done" to "delicious." (Pictured on page 199).

SERVES 2 OR 3

1 pound (450 g) firm zucchini, cut crosswise into slices ⅜ inch (1 cm) thick (cut on the diagonal so the slices have a larger diameter)

Extra-virgin olive oil

Kosher salt

Freshly ground black pepper

2 tablespoons finely chopped garlic

1 tablespoon chopped fresh thyme or rosemary (or a mix)

1 pound (450 g) firm slicing tomatoes, such as Early Girl, cut into slices ¼ inch (6 mm) thick

1 cup (100 g) finely grated Parmigiano-Reggiano cheese

¼ cup (7 g) finely sliced fresh basil leaves

Preheat the oven to 425°F (220°C).

Toss the zucchini with about 2 tablespoons olive oil, ½ teaspoon salt, a few twists of black pepper, the garlic, and thyme. If the tomato slices are larger than about 2 inches (5 cm) across, cut them in half.

Arrange a row of zucchini slices across a gratin or shallow baking dish, overlapping them slightly and standing them up on their edge; they'll want to slide down, but as the pan fills, the vegetables will cooperate more. Next arrange a row of tomato slices, overlapping each other and the zucchini. Sprinkle with a big pinch of the Parmigiano and a pinch of the basil. Repeat with rows of zucchini and tomato, adding the cheese in between, until everything's in the dish. You'll probably need to scooch the vegetables tighter together, sliding them so they're almost vertical rather than lying down in the dish, in order to get everything in, depending on the size of your dish. If you have any cheese and/or basil left, distribute it over the gratin.

Cook the gratin uncovered until the vegetables are tender and the juices are bubbling and browned around the edges of the dish, 35 to 40 minutes. Let the dish rest for at least 10 minutes so the juices redistribute and thicken; this rest will make the final consistency much better than if you ate it immediately. Serve warm.

Or Try This Idea

Per Susie's original, slice a large onion, season it lightly with salt and pepper, and cook it slowly in olive oil until it's very soft, sweet, and starting to caramelize, about 20 minutes. Spread the onion in the gratin dish, then proceed with the recipe.

My Time-Consuming-but-Worth-It Ratatouille

So many ratatouille recipes seem to me like nothing more than a potful of stewed vegetables, tasty enough but with undefined flavors. The main advantage of that style of ratatouille is that the dish is mostly hands-off.

This version is the opposite of hands-off. It takes a bit of time and effort to make (though is it really an effort to spend time in the kitchen cooking beautiful seasonal produce?), but the result—a jumble of glistening vegetables that have each been cooked to bring out their best features, dressed with a bright and fruity vegetable glaze—is so worth it. You'll use a lot of olive oil, so the dish feels almost like a vegetable confit or caponata. You can serve it as a side dish, of course, but I bet you'll find endless things to do with this ratatouille, which lasts for a week in the fridge; see the ideas at the end of the recipe.

SERVES 6 TO 8, DEPENDING ON HOW YOU'RE SERVING IT

About 1 pound (450 g) eggplant, peeled and cut into 1-inch (2.5 cm) chunks

Kosher salt

Extra-virgin olive oil

About 2 cups (225 g) thinly sliced onion

2 teaspoons chopped fresh thyme

2 medium red bell peppers (about 1 pound/450 g), peeled as much as possible with a vegetable peeler and cut into ¾-inch (1 cm) pieces

2 teaspoons chopped fresh rosemary

1 pound (450 g) firm zucchini or other summer squash (3 or 4 small), halved lengthwise and cut crosswise into half-moons ⅛ inch (3 mm) thick

¼ cup (25 g) chopped garlic (6 to 8 large cloves)

continues

Toss the eggplant with 1 teaspoon kosher salt, pile into a colander, and let sit in the sink or over a bowl while you prepare the other vegetables.

Note that you're going to be sautéing all the vegetables in succession, which should create a nice layer of browned vegetable juices in the bottom of the skillet as you go. But if you see that the vegetable juices are burning, rinse the pan before cooking the next vegetable. Better to miss out on a few juices than to have the ratatouille bitter.

Set another colander or a large sieve over a bowl to catch the juices. The accumulated juices from all the vegetables will become a delicious glaze to finish the dish. In a 12-inch (30 cm) skillet, heat 2 tablespoons olive oil over medium heat. Add the onion, thyme, and ¼ teaspoon salt. Cook, stirring occasionally, until the onion is very soft and deep golden brown, 15 to 20 minutes. Scrape into the colander.

In the same skillet, heat another 3 tablespoons oil over medium-high heat. Add the bell peppers and ¼ teaspoon salt. Cook, stirring occasionally, until they start to soften and get browned around the edges, about 5 minutes. Add the rosemary, reduce the heat to medium, and cook, stirring occasionally, until the peppers are extremely soft and sweet, another 10 to 15 minutes. Add to the onion in the colander.

Heat another 1 tablespoon oil over high heat, and as soon as you see the first hint of smoke, add the zucchini and ¼ teaspoon salt. Shake and stir to distribute the zucchini slices evenly in the pan so they all get browned. Reduce the

1 pound (450 g) tomatoes, cored and cut into 1-inch (2.5 cm) chunks

1 teaspoon finely grated lemon zest

1 tablespoon fresh lemon juice

Hot sauce

2 tablespoons thinly sliced fresh basil leaves

2 tablespoons roughly chopped fresh flat-leaf parsley

1 tablespoon thinly sliced fresh mint leaves

heat to medium and cook until they are tender and nicely browned on both sides, 5 to 7 minutes. Add to the colander with the onion and peppers.

Blot the eggplant with paper towels. Heat 3 tablespoons olive oil in the skillet over high heat, add the eggplant, and shake and stir to distribute evenly in the pan so it all gets browned. Adjust the heat to medium-high and cook until the eggplant is lightly browned on several surfaces, about 5 minutes. Reduce the heat to medium and cook until the eggplant is very tender—not at all al dente—another 13 to 15 minutes. Add to the other vegetables.

Add 1 or 2 more tablespoons olive oil to the pan and heat over medium-high heat. Add the garlic and let sizzle for about 30 seconds, then add the tomatoes and all their juices and ¼ teaspoon salt. Cook until the tomatoes collapse slightly and the juices thicken and darken a bit, 3 to 5 minutes. As you're cooking, scrape the bottom of the pan to deglaze all the cooked-on vegetable juices. Add to the colander, scraping out all the juices from the skillet. Gently fold everything together and let the vegetables sit in the colander for 15 to 20 minutes.

At that point, around ½ cup (120 ml) liquid should have accumulated in the bowl. Pour it into a small saucepan, heat until gently boiling, and boil until the liquid is reduced to about ¼ cup (60 ml). The flavor should be very bright and intense. Add the lemon zest, lemon juice, and a little hot sauce to taste. Transfer the vegetables to a bowl and fold in the glaze, along with the basil, parsley, and mint. Taste for salt and add more if needed.

Serve soon, if you want the ratatouille to be warm, or let it cool and serve at room temperature.

Or Try These Ideas

OMELET FILLING: Tuck a few spoonfuls of ratatouille into an omelet with goat cheese.

BRUSCHETTA TOPPING: Pile some ratatouille onto slices of grilled bread.

POLENTA TOPPING: Sauce a bowl of creamy polenta or fried polenta squares with ratatouille and shower with grated pecorino.

PASTA SAUCE: Toss the ratatouille with a cooked chunky pasta such as rigatoni and add a handful of torn basil leaves.

White Beans with Tomato Confit and Herbs

The flavor combination of creamy beans and bright umami-rich tomatoes is unbeatable, but I don't usually cook dried beans with tomatoes in the pot because the acid in the tomatoes can inhibit the bean from softening. The solution is to simmer the beans in one pot, make a mirepoix of aromatic vegetables in another pan into which you fold roasted or confit tomatoes, and then marry the two in the serving bowl.

SERVES 4 TO 6

Extra-virgin olive oil

6 garlic cloves

Chile flakes

1 onion

1 pound (450 g) dried white beans, such as cannellini, Zolfini, or Great Northern

1 bay leaf

Kosher salt

2 medium celery stalks, finely chopped

1 large carrot, finely chopped

1 small or ½ large fennel bulb, trimmed and finely chopped (optional)

1 tablespoon chopped fresh thyme or rosemary (or a mix)

Freshly ground black pepper

2 cups Cherry Tomato Confit (page 231), Classic Roasted Tomatoes (page 48), or Blasted Cherry Tomatoes (page 151)

½ cup (15 g) roughly chopped fresh flat-leaf parsley or basil (or a mix)

In a large Dutch oven or other deep heavy-bottomed pot, heat a generous glug of olive oil over medium heat. Smash 3 of the garlic cloves, peel, and add to the oil, along with a pinch of chile flakes. Cook the garlic gently until it becomes very fragrant and light golden but not actually browned, about 4 minutes.

Cut a thick slice from the onion and add it to the pot. It will break up during cooking, so no need to chop it in any particular way. Add the beans, bay leaf, 2 teaspoons salt, and water (or broth, if you prefer) to cover by 2 inches (5 cm). Bring the beans to a simmer, cover the pot, and adjust the heat so they simmer very gently. You don't ever want the beans to boil rapidly, which can break them up, especially as they get closer to being tender.

Cook until the beans are fully tender (be sure to taste several of them) but haven't yet started falling apart. This could take from 1 hour to 3 hours, depending on the age and type of bean. Once the beans are tender, pull them from the heat. Taste them again, and if they need more salt, stir it in now. Let the beans cool in their liquid.

While the beans are cooking, finely chop the rest of the onion and the remaining 3 (peeled) garlic cloves. In a large skillet, heat a generous glug of olive oil over medium heat. Add the onion, garlic, celery, carrot, fennel (if using), and thyme. Season generously with salt and black pepper. Cook, stirring frequently, until the vegetables are fragrant, tender, and lightly golden but not actually browned, 10 to 12 minutes.

Fold in the tomatoes and cook just long enough to warm through, but don't let them disintegrate—you're not making a sauce; you're making more like a compote. Taste and adjust the seasoning with more chile flakes, salt, and/or black pepper.

If the beans are in a lot of liquid, drain some off so that they are wet and sloppy but not swimming; reserve the excess bean liquor (I love that phrase) to use in a soup or other dish.

To serve, if your bean cooking pot is attractive enough for the table, spoon the warm tomato mixture onto the top and finish with the parsley and a drizzle of olive oil. Or transfer the beans to a serving bowl and add the tomatoes, parsley, and olive oil. The beans are best when warm but not hot.

Or Try These Ideas

PARMIGIANO: Add a small piece of Parmigiano rind to the beans as they cook; be sure to retrieve what's left of it before serving, though quite a lot will have melted.

SAUSAGES: Brown some sausages (Italian, kielbasa, bratwurst), cut into pieces, and add to the cooked beans before you add the tomatoes.

PANCETTA: Cook some chopped pancetta with the onion, celery, and carrot mixture.

Tomato Tarts and Pastries

Tomato Tart with Ricotta and Herbs

This tart is a perfect balance between buttery crust and creamy-but-light filling of ricotta, fresh herbs, and thinly sliced fresh tomato. Any flavorful tomato that's not super juicy will work well (see below for instructions on dealing with the juice), but you'll get the prettiest look if you use a mix of colors. If your tomato slices have a large diameter, cut them in half so they fit better in your tart shell. (Pictured on page 212)

MAKES ONE 9- OR 10-INCH (23 OR 25 CM) TART

Flaky Pastry Dough (recipe follows)

All-purpose flour, for dusting

About 1 pound (450 g) firm-ripe tomatoes

Kosher salt

1 cup (240 g) whole-milk ricotta (see Notes)

1 cup (100 g) finely grated Parmigiano-Reggiano cheese

1 egg

Pinch of freshly grated nutmeg

Freshly ground black pepper

¼ cup (7 g) lightly packed finely chopped fresh mint, basil, or flat-leaf parsley

NOTES

- This tart reheats beautifully, so be sure to reserve at least one piece to enjoy the next day. Reheat leftovers on a baking sheet in a 375°F (190°C) oven until the pastry has re-crisped and the filling is warm, about 10 minutes.

- Look for a ricotta with a looser, creamier texture than that of many mainstream brands, which can have a pasty consistency. Bellwether Farms' "basket ricotta" is luscious; Calabro and Organic Valley are also decent choices.

Take the dough from the fridge and let it sit at room temperature to soften it slightly, which will help minimize cracking and ripping as you roll it out. Place a 9- or 10-inch (23 or 25 cm) tart pan with a removable bottom on a baking sheet (to make it easier to transport the tart into and out of the oven).

Lightly flour the work surface and roll the dough to a 12-inch (30 cm) round. Transfer the dough to the tart pan by gently rolling it onto the rolling pin, moving it so you're right over the pan, and then unrolling the dough into the pan, draping it so you can position it without ripping or stretching. Lift the edges of the dough to give you enough slack to line the sides of the pan without stretching the dough. Press the dough onto the bottom and sides of the pan.

Trim off excess dough, leaving about ½ inch (1.25 cm) beyond the top of the pan. Fold the excess over and press the dough against the sides of the pan so the edges of the crust are thick and neat and rise just a bit above the edge. Chill for at least 30 minutes. (You can prep the crust to this point, wrap it well, and freeze it for up to 1 month. If baking from the frozen state, don't thaw; just add a few minutes to the baking time.)

Preheat the oven to 400°F (200°C).

To blind-bake the crust, line the tart shell with parchment or foil and fill it with pie weights or dried beans, pushing them into the corner between the bottom and sides so the edges don't puff or slump too much. Bake the crust until the edges seem firm and slightly dry and are beginning to color, about 10 minutes. Don't let the crust actually brown.

Remove the crust from the oven and take out the pie weights and parchment. Reduce the oven temperature to 325°F (160°C) and return the crust to the oven. Bake until the center of the crust looks dry, about 20 minutes more. Let the crust cool completely on a cooling rack while you prepare the rest of the ingredients. Increase the oven temperature to 350°F (180°C).

While the crust is cooling, cut the tomatoes into ¼-inch (6 mm) slices and arrange the tomato slices on a cooling rack set over a sheet pan to catch the drips. If you don't have a cooling rack, just spread them out on the sheet pan. Sprinkle with a bit of salt and let drain.

In a food processor, combine the ricotta, half the Parmigiano, the egg, nutmeg, and a pinch each of salt and black pepper and pulse to blend (you can also do this with a whisk or mixer). When it's nice and creamy, pulse in the herbs. Spread the ricotta filling into the cooled crust.

Blot the tomatoes thoroughly with paper towels and arrange in a pretty pattern on the ricotta, overlapping the slices slightly. Bake the tart for about 30 minutes, then sprinkle the remaining Parmigiano on the surface and keep baking until the filling looks slightly puffy, the tomatoes look dry, and the cheese is starting to brown a bit, another 20 to 30 minutes. If the crust is browning too much at any time during cooking, reduce the oven temperature a bit.

Cool the tart on a rack and serve warm or at room temperature.

continues

FLAKY PASTRY DOUGH

A stand mixer makes this dough super easy, but you can also make it entirely by hand. I give both methods below.

MAKES ENOUGH FOR ONE 9- OR 10-INCH (23 OR 25 CM) TART

1½ cups (195 g) unbleached all-purpose flour, plus more for dusting

½ teaspoon kosher salt

8 tablespoons (115 g) very cold unsalted butter, cut into cubes

¼ cup (60 ml) ice water, or more as needed

Stand Mixer Method

Combine the flour, salt, and butter in a stand mixer fitted with the paddle. Mix on low until the butter is flattened a bit and the pieces are about half their original size. With the mixer running, slowly pour a bit more than half of the water into the flour and butter and mix until the dough barely holds together; it will look quite shaggy. Take a big pinch and give it a squeeze. If it holds together and feels moist, you're good. If it feels a bit dry or powdery, pulse in a few more drops of water.

By-Hand Method

In a wide bowl, toss together the flour, salt, and butter. Pinch and press the mixture with your fingers to encourage the butter to form smaller flattened pieces. Gradually add about half the ice water while tossing the flour mixture with your fingers or a fork to evenly distribute the water. Don't add all the water until you're sure you need it. Test by taking a big pinch of the dough. If it holds together and feels moist, you're good. If it feels a bit dry or powdery, toss in a few more drops of water.

For Both Methods

When the dough is the right consistency, dump it onto a lightly floured work surface. Knead it gently by pushing sections of the dough away from you with the heel of your hand, almost like you're smearing the dough into the work surface (but don't get carried away!). Gather it back together, using a bench scraper if you have one. This will distribute the butter in a way that creates a very tender dough. After a few strokes, the dough should feel like it's coming together; it doesn't need to be perfectly smooth at this point. Shape the dough into a flat disk, wrap in plastic, and refrigerate for about 30 minutes, or wrap up a bit more and freeze for up to 3 months.

Roasted-Tomato Puff Pastry Appetizer . . . with Options

Here a simple strip of puff pastry becomes a platform for roasted tomatoes and other savory morsels. The dough (store-bought frozen or from-scratch "rough puff," which is super easy and fun to make) bakes up flaky and delicate, yet it's sturdy enough to handle the juicy consistency of roasted tomatoes. Make an array of these flat tarts with various toppings and serve several on a big cutting board. Cut a few slices to give guests the idea and then let people cut their own from there.

MAKES TWO 6-BY-14-INCH (15 BY 35 CM) TARTS; SERVES 8 AS AN APPETIZER

All-purpose flour, for dusting

1 sheet (about 9 ounces/250 g) frozen puff pastry, thawed (or ½ recipe Super-Flaky "Almost" Puff Pastry Dough, page 226)

About 20 Classic Roasted Tomato halves (page 48)

3 ounces (85 g) fresh goat cheese

Extra-virgin olive oil (optional)

Preheat the oven to 425°F (220°C) and line a baking sheet with parchment or a silicone baking mat.

On a lightly floured counter, roll the pastry to a 12-by-14-inch (30 by 35 cm) rectangle. Cut it into two 6-by-14-inch (15 by 35 cm) strips. Transfer the strips to the baking sheet (use two baking sheets if the strips are crowded). Prick each strip with a fork at ½-inch (1.25 cm) intervals, leaving about a ½-inch (1.25 cm) border unpricked. This will help keep the center area from puffing up too much; ironically, you don't want the puff pastry to actually puff! Bake until the pastry is light gold and starting to dry out, about 10 minutes.

Remove the baking sheet from the oven, press down any puffiness in the center of the strips, and arrange the tomatoes in an even layer on the pastry (a few gaps are fine). Return to the oven and continue baking until the pastry is golden brown (be sure to check the underside also), the borders are puffed, and the tomatoes are hot, another 12 to 15 minutes.

Remove the baking sheet from the oven, crumble the goat cheese over the tarts, and slide the tarts onto a cooling rack. Brush the edges with olive oil, if you like, and cool for about 10 minutes, then slide the tarts onto a cutting board and cut crosswise into servings, 2 to 3 inches (5 to 7.5 cm). Serve warm or at room temperature.

Or Try These Ideas

LEEK AND HERB: Split 1 small leek (about 9 ounces/255 g) lengthwise, rinse well, and cut into half-moons ¼ inch (6 mm) thick. Sauté the leek in 1 tablespoon butter with a pinch of chile flakes and ½ teaspoon kosher salt, stirring frequently, until very soft and sweet but not at all browned, 10 to 15 minutes. Fold in about 2 tablespoons chopped fresh herbs (such as tarragon, dill, chervil, parsley, chives, or basil, or a mix). Scrape the leeks onto a plate to cool. Before adding the tomatoes to the pastry, spread the leeks in an even layer on both tarts, then top with the tomatoes and continue with the recipe as written.

BACON AND BLUE CHEESE: Bake the pastry and top with the tomatoes as directed. About 5 minutes before you think the tarts are done (about 10 minutes after you top the pastry with the tomatoes), crumble 4 strips of cooked-until-crisp bacon and about 3 ounces (85 g) blue cheese over the tarts (omit the goat cheese). Return to the oven to finish cooking, letting the bacon warm up and the cheese get slightly melty.

DIJON, HAM, AND FONTINA: Bake the pastry for 10 minutes, and then, before adding the tomatoes, spread it with a thin layer of Dijon (or other tasty) mustard. Distribute 3 ounces (85 g) shredded Fontina cheese over the mustard (omitting the goat cheese), then top with the roasted tomatoes. Top the tomatoes with about 3 ounces (85 g) cooked ham (such as honey-roasted or Black Forest ham that you'd get at the deli counter), cut into thin julienne strips. Return the tarts to the oven to finish cooking, letting the ham heat up and the cheese get slightly melty.

HARISSA AND BLACK OLIVE: Bake the pastry for 10 minutes, and then, before adding the tomatoes, spread it with a thin layer of harissa (a North African chile and paprika condiment). Top with the tomatoes (omit the goat cheese). Distribute about ¼ cup (45 g) chopped pitted black olives, preferably oil-cured, over the tomatoes. Note: These can be very salty, so chop them fine.

Tomato-Gruyère Galette with Walnut Crust

For cooks like me who aren't the most skilled at fine pastry techniques, a galette is a godsend. If your galette ends up more oval than round and your pleating is uneven, don't stress—it's not messy, it's rustic!

The dough for this galette is rustic as well, with the addition of ground walnuts and some whole-grain flour. The walnuts make the dough a bit friable (easily crumbled), so don't worry if it rips; just pinch it back together.

While you can make the dough by hand, you'll need a processor to chop the walnuts fine enough; chopping by hand will leave them too coarse, making the dough too rough. If you don't have a food processor, use the Flaky Pastry Dough (page 216) and sprinkle the galette with chopped walnuts during the last 10 minutes of cooking.

MAKES ONE 12-INCH (30 CM) GALETTE

1 to 1¼ pounds (450 to 565 g) tomatoes, cored and cut into slices ¼ inch (6 mm) thick

Kosher salt

Walnut Pâte Brisée (recipe follows)

All-purpose flour, for dusting

2 tablespoons Dijon mustard

2 tablespoons crème fraîche or heavy cream

Freshly ground black pepper

1 cup (120 g) shredded Gruyère cheese

1 tablespoon (15 g) butter, cut into bits

Preheat the oven to 425°F (220°C). Line a large baking sheet with parchment paper.

Put the tomato slices on a cooling rack set over a sheet pan to catch the drips. (If you don't have a rack, just spread them out on the sheet pan.) Sprinkle with a little salt and let drain at least 20 minutes.

Roll the dough on a lightly floured surface to a 15-inch (38 cm) round. Transfer it to the baking sheet by gently rolling the dough up around the rolling pin and unrolling it onto the parchment. The dough will overhang the baking sheet, but it will fit once you fold it.

In a small bowl, stir together the mustard and crème fraîche; spread it all over the dough except for a 1½-inch (4 cm) border. Season generously with black pepper. Distribute the Gruyère over the mustard, making sure you go all the way to the edges of the border.

Blot the tomatoes aggressively with paper towels, but don't smash them. Arrange the tomato slices in a pretty pattern on the cheese, bringing them all the way to the border of the crust. (I emphasize this because you don't want bites that are all crust, no filling.) Fold the dough border over the tomatoes, pleating the excess as you work your way around the galette. If the dough rips a bit, just pinch it back together. Dot the surface of the tomatoes with the butter.

Bake until the crust is a rich brown—on the border and also the underside—and the tomatoes are dryish and starting to brown and bubble a bit, 40 to 50 minutes.

Cool the galette, slice, and serve warm but not hot.

continues

WALNUT PÂTE BRISÉE

MAKES ENOUGH FOR ONE 12-INCH (30 CM) GALETTE

⅓ cup (30 g) walnut halves

2 cups (260 g) 50/50 mix of all-purpose and whole-grain flour (or all all-purpose), plus more for dusting

½ teaspoon kosher salt

12 tablespoons (170 g) very cold unsalted butter, cut into pieces

¼ cup (60 ml) ice water

In a food processor, pulse the walnuts until they are very finely ground, but take care not to process them so much that they become walnut butter.

Add the flour and salt to the food processor and pulse to blend.

Add the butter and pulse until the largest piece of butter is the size of a small pea.

Drizzle in some of the ice water, continuing to pulse so the water doesn't all get absorbed in one spot. As you add the water, watch the dough: When the flour mixture starts to climb up the sides of the processor bowl, stop. Open the bowl and squeeze a big pinch of the dough (be careful with the processor blade). If it holds together and feels moist, you're good. If it feels a bit dry or powdery, pulse in a few more drops of water.

When the dough is the right consistency, dump it onto a lightly floured work surface and knead it lightly by pushing sections of the dough away from you with the heel of your hand and then gathering it back together, using a bench scraper if you have one. This helps distribute the butter so it creates a very tender dough. After a few strokes, shape it into a flat disk. Wrap the dough in plastic and refrigerate for about 30 minutes, or wrap up a bit more and freeze for up to 3 months.

Tomato, Turkey, and Havarti Turnovers

Turnovers are the perfect travel food. Make them when you're hitting the road and heading to a river, mountain, or campsite—any type of outing where portability is as critical as deliciousness. Despite the pastry being super flaky, these turnovers are sturdy enough to wrap in foil and stick in a backpack or ski jacket.

I like using spicy Tomato Jam #2 and slices of fresh tomato, plus whatever cheese and/or meat I have on hand, as the jam brings some spice heat and the tomato adds a hit of freshness. But Classic Roasted Tomatoes (page 48), Cherry Tomato Confit (page 231), or Low and Slow Roasted Plum Tomatoes (page 165) would also be delicious in the filling.

MAKES 8 TO 10 TURNOVERS

Super-Flaky "Almost" Puff Pastry Dough (page 226)

All-purpose flour, for dusting

3 to 4 tablespoons Tomato Jam #2 (page 57)

8 ounces (225 g) Havarti or other mild but firm cheese, shredded

½ pound (225 g) thinly sliced roast turkey (from the deli is fine)

8 to 10 very thin slices tomato, more if the diameter of the slices is small

Let the dough warm up at room temperature for about 20 minutes if it has been in the refrigerator for longer than 30 minutes.

Line a baking sheet with parchment paper or a silicone baking mat. Arrange your filling ingredients in a handy place so that you can efficiently roll the dough, fill, shape, and place the turnovers on the baking sheet.

Cut the block of dough in half (it's easier to handle this way) and lightly flour a work surface.

Roll one piece of the dough until it's about ⅛ inch (3 mm) thick. The shape of your dough doesn't matter, because you will be cutting out rounds, but aim for even thickness throughout. Using a saucer or other disk about 5 inches (12.5 cm) in diameter as a guide, cut out as many rounds of dough as you can. You want at least 4 from each dough half; you can reroll the dough scraps.

Spread one round with a thin layer of tomato jam (about 1 teaspoon), leaving a ½-inch (1.25 cm) border, then arrange some cheese, turkey, and a fresh tomato slice on one half of the round. With your finger or a pastry brush, moisten the border of dough with water and then fold the "empty" half of the dough over the filling to make a half-moon turnover. Gently press the border to seal and then crimp the edges by pressing with a fork, or use whatever crimping method you like. Transfer to the baking sheet and continue with the rest of the dough and filling.

Refrigerate the turnovers for at least 30 minutes, and up to 2 hours (if you're chilling longer than 30 minutes, cover the turnovers loosely with plastic wrap or a cloth so they don't dry out too much).

Meanwhile, preheat the oven to 375°F (190°C).

When you're ready to bake, cut three slits in the top of each turnover, to release steam during cooking (this prevents the dough from bursting in annoying ways). Bake until the dough is nicely golden brown all over (check the undersides) and the filling is bubbling slightly through the vents or at the edges, 30 to 40 minutes. Let the turnovers cool for a few minutes and then eat warm or at room temperature. These reheat nicely.

Or Try This Idea

HAM AND DIJON: Omit the tomato jam and brush the dough with Dijon mustard instead. Swap out the turkey for ham.

RATATOUILLE: Omit the tomato jam, ham, and tomato slices and add a spoonful of ratatouille (see page 207).

ROASTED TOMATO: Substitute Classic Roasted Tomatoes (page 48) for the fresh slices.

Super-Flaky "Almost" Puff Pastry Dough

This pastry is called "rough puff" (or demi-feuilletage in French), and it's a good one to have in your repertoire. A million times easier to make than classic puff pastry, it is nonetheless delicate and super flaky, and though the flakes aren't organized in the structured way of an actual puff pastry, I think that makes it more versatile to use as a crust for pies or tarts, and, of course, as the dough for turnovers. Plus, this dough is fun to make.

Many people have anxiety about making pie dough, which is understandable, because getting the moisture wrong or overworking the dough can result in a hard-to-wrangle dough or a tough tart shell. But I guarantee that if you follow the instructions (and measure your flour carefully, ideally weighing it on a scale), you will be thrilled with this "almost" puff pastry. The dough freezes well, so make a double batch and use it for any pastry for which you want a very flaky dough.

A quick explanation of the process before you begin: Unlike with pie doughs in which the goal is to turn the butter into tiny bits so the dough is crumbly and tender, here you want the butter to be in small, flat sheets. The great American baker and cookbook author Jim Dodge once described the butter pieces as looking like paint chips, which is a helpful—though not appetizing—image. You press the butter into the flour until you have well-distributed flakes of butter. At that point, you start a series of actions that spreads the butter even thinner and integrates it more deeply with the flour. After a few of these rolls and turns (explained below), the dough starts to cohere into something smooth and workable, and you will even be able to see the fine layers of butter and flour in the cross section of the block of finished dough.

MAKES ABOUT 1 POUND (450 G) DOUGH

1¾ cups (225 g) all-purpose flour, plus more for dusting

½ teaspoon kosher salt

8 ounces (2 sticks/225 g) cold unsalted butter, cut into ½-inch (1.25 cm) cubes

Up to ½ cup (120 ml) ice water

Clear a space on the counter to work with the dough. Put the flour and salt in a wide bowl and whisk to mix (choose a large enough bowl that you can fluff the flour around without it spilling out).

Add the butter cubes and toss the butter and flour together. Pinch and press the mixture with your fingers to encourage the butter to form small, flattened pieces.

When you like the consistency of the butter and flour—meaning all the butter is flattened—sprinkle in about 3 tablespoons ice water, fluffing the flour as you do so that the water gets distributed. Pinch a big wad of dough and see whether it holds together or if it's still sort of powdery. If it's powdery, sprinkle on more water, distributing it as best you can. Pinch the dough again, continuing to fluff in a bit more water as needed until the dough is moist enough to hold together. Try not to add more water than necessary; you may not use the entire ½ cup (120 ml).

Lightly flour the counter and dump out the dough. Scoot it into a rough rectangle shape with a short side facing you, and press on it with your rolling pin to compact the flour and butter a bit. Now start rolling it. Just ignore the fact that it's a pile of butter and flour and not an actual dough yet.

When you've rolled it out a bit—and, yes, it will be a mess—slide a bench scraper under the flour mix and fold the rectangle back onto itself in thirds, like you're folding a letter. (Do you remember letters?) Now turn the rectangle 90 degrees so a short side is in front of you again (even if it's not holding together, just pretend it is) and roll again. Continue rolling out and folding, scooting the runaway bits of flour or butter back into the main block, until the dough feels smoother and more pliable; this should happen after about four rolls-and-folds, once you get over the initial pile-of-flour stage.

Once your dough is smooth and you don't see any more huge chunks of butter in it, wrap it in plastic and let it sit for about 30 minutes. This will allow the flour to fully hydrate and will make the dough easier to work with. (Note: If you roll the dough too much, you'll develop a lot of gluten, which will make the dough very elastic and hard to roll out.)

You can keep the dough in the refrigerator for up to 2 days, or freeze it at this point, wrapped really well. The dough will last nicely in the freezer for up to 3 months.

Tomato Tart with Parmigiano Frangipane

I love using traditional frangipane in fruit tarts because the almond-butter-sugar-egg filling not only brings richness to the pastry but also absorbs the fruit juices during cooking, keeping the crust crisp. But even though tomatoes are botanically a fruit, they don't play well in dessert-y fruit tarts, so I adapted this classic frangipane recipe to make it savory.

Serve the tart with a green salad for brunch or a light supper, or as part of what my mother used to call "heavy hors d'oeuvres," meaning an array of snacks that were substantial enough to prevent my parents' guests from getting too tipsy after a couple of Manhattans. You can make the pastry and line the tart pan and then freeze it up to a month ahead. When you're ready to serve, fill the still-frozen tart shell with the frangipane, add your tomatoes, invite the neighbors, and break out the bourbon.

MAKES ONE 10-INCH (25 CM) TART

Flaky Pastry Dough (page 216)

All-purpose flour, for dusting

Parmigiano Frangipane

⅔ cup (65 g) raw or very lightly toasted walnuts, almonds (skin-on is fine), or pecans

½ cup (50 g) freshly grated Parmigiano-Reggiano cheese

6 tablespoons (90 g) butter, at room temperature

2 tablespoons all-purpose flour

½ teaspoon kosher salt

Pinch of Aleppo pepper or cayenne (optional)

2 eggs, beaten

About 24 tomatoes from Cherry Tomato Confit (page 231), well drained, or 12 to 15 fresh cherry tomatoes, halved

Take the dough from the fridge and let it sit at room temperature to soften it slightly, which will help minimize cracking and ripping as you roll it out. Place a 9- or 10-inch (23 or 25 cm) tart pan with a removable bottom on a baking sheet (to make it easier to transport the tart into and out of the oven).

Lightly flour the work surface and roll the dough to a 12- to 13-inch (30 to 33 cm) round. Transfer the dough to the tart pan by gently rolling it up onto the rolling pin, moving it so you're right over the pan, and then unrolling the dough into the pan, draping it so you can position it without ripping or stretching. Lift the edges of the dough to give you enough slack to line the sides of the pan without stretching the dough. Gently press the dough onto the bottom and sides of the pan.

Fold the excess dough over and press the dough against the sides of the pan so the edges of the crust are thick and neat and rise just a bit above the edge. Chill for at least 30 minutes. (You can prep the crust to this point, wrap it well, and freeze it for up to 1 month. If baking from the frozen state, don't thaw, just add a few minutes to the baking time.)

Preheat the oven to 400°F (200°C).

To blind-bake the crust, prick the dough all over using a fork, spacing the perforations about 1 inch (2.5 cm) apart. This will keep the crust from puffing too much during baking. Line the tart shell with parchment or foil and fill it with pie weights or dried beans, pushing them into the corners between bottom and sides so the edges don't puff or slump too much. Bake the crust until the edges seem firm and slightly dry and are beginning to color, about 10 minutes. Don't let the crust actually brown.

Remove the crust from the oven and take out the pie weights and parchment. Reduce the oven temperature to 325°F (160°C) and return the crust to the oven. Bake until the center of the crust looks dry, about 20 minutes more. Let cool completely on a rack while you prepare the rest of the ingredients. Increase the oven temperature to 350°F (180°C).

MAKE THE PARMIGIANO FRANGIPANE: In a food processor, pulse the walnuts until they are finely ground, but be sure to stop before they head into walnut-butter territory. Add the Parmigiano, softened butter, flour, salt, and Aleppo pepper (if using) and pulse until you have a fairly smooth paste.

Add the eggs and process until smooth. Spread the frangipane in an even layer in the crust. Place the tomatoes on top in a single layer in a pretty pattern, with a bit of space between them so the frangipane is exposed. If using fresh cherry tomatoes, arrange them cut side up.

Transfer the tart to the oven and bake until the crust is nicely browned, the frangipane is golden brown and puffy, and the tomatoes are bubbling, 30 to 40 minutes. Cool the tart, on a rack if possible, and serve warm or at room temperature. The tart is best eaten soon after baking, but you can reheat it in a 375°F (190°C) oven just until warmed through.

CHERRY TOMATO CONFIT

You are probably most familiar with the confit technique—
slowly cooking an ingredient in fat until tender and semi-
preserved—as it relates to duck, but tomatoes also benefit
from the method. The flesh softens and absorbs the flavor
of the olive oil and whatever seasonings you use. When you
have an abundance of cherry tomatoes, especially different
colors and shapes, toss them into a heavy pot with herbs and
garlic, float on some good olive oil, and walk away from the
stove; in about an hour you'll have a juicy, bright condiment
to use in grain salads, on pasta, as a pizza topping, or even on
its own as a companion to grilled meat or fish. And the bonus
is the flavored oil, which is delicious as a finishing oil or as a
component in a vinaigrette.

Managing the Variables

Unlike with Blasted Cherry Tomatoes (page 151), the goal is not to burst open the tomatoes nor to caramelize them, but rather to simply soften and sweeten the flesh and allow it to take on the flavors of the oil and seasonings. A little bit of browning around the edges of the tomatoes as they cook is fine, but the main thing you'll need to do as you cook these is to manage the sizzle. If you hear a lot of sizzle, reduce the temperature just a bit.

CHERRY TOMATO CONFIT

MAKES AS MANY AS WILL FIT INTO YOUR POT

Cherry tomatoes (a mix of colors is ideal), stems removed

Extra-virgin olive oil

1 or 2 garlic cloves, smashed

Small sprigs fresh rosemary and/or thyme

Pinch of chile flakes (optional)

Cut any large tomatoes in half and arrange all the tomatoes, cut side up, in a heavy-bottomed pot, such as a Dutch oven. Add enough olive oil so it comes a little less than halfway up the sides of the tomatoes. Toss in the garlic, rosemary, and chile flakes (if using).

Cook over very low heat at a bare simmer until the tomatoes are soft and slightly wrinkled, the bottoms are just barely browned, and the oil is flavored with tomato juice and seasonings, about 1 hour. Let cool in the oil.

Transfer to a jar or other airtight container and store in the refrigerator for up to 2 weeks.

Good Things to Do with Cherry Tomato Confit

Stuff into a pita with feta, chopped cucumber, and tahini dressing; toss with capers and chopped fresh mint and top grilled lamb chops; top grilled bread spread with ricotta; stir into warm white beans; fold with cooked penne pasta, chickpeas, and diced mozzarella.

Cherry Tomato Clafoutis

A clafoutis is a simple rustic French batter pudding that is traditionally made with cherries . . . so why not cherry tomatoes? It's quick to make, and while the sweet cherry version is served for dessert, the savory cherry tomato version would be delicious for brunch, as a light lunch, or as a side dish to rosemary-flecked roast chicken or lamb chops from the grill.

Cherry tomatoes are juicier than the dark sweet cherries used in classic clafoutis, so a thicker batter will better absorb the juices. The idea is to have a contrast between eggy, crepe-like batter and bright, juicy tomatoes. A mix of colors looks spectacular, so aim for at least two types of cherry tomato.

SERVES 4

Butter or oil, for the pie pan

3 large eggs

⅔ cup (160 ml) whole milk

½ cup (65 g) all-purpose flour

½ cup (50 g) finely grated Parmigiano-Reggiano cheese

2 tablespoons melted browned butter (see page 155)

¼ cup (7 g) lightly packed finely chopped tender fresh herbs, such as flat-leaf parsley, dill, basil, or tarragon (or a mix)

1 teaspoon finely chopped fresh thyme

1 teaspoon kosher salt

Big pinch of Aleppo pepper or chile flakes

Freshly ground black pepper

½ pound (225 g) cherry tomatoes, a mix of colors if possible

Preheat the oven to 350°F (180°C). Grease a 9-inch (23 cm) glass or ceramic pie pan with butter or oil.

In a large bowl, whisk the eggs until nicely blended, then whisk in the milk. Whisk in the flour a bit at a time, trying to avoid lumps but not freaking out if things look lumpy. They will resolve themselves as the clafoutis cooks.

Whisk in the grated Parmigiano, the browned butter, chopped tender herbs, thyme, salt, Aleppo pepper, and several twists of black pepper.

Pile the tomatoes into the pie pan, pour on the batter, and try to spread out the tomatoes so they are evenly distributed, though they'll likely want to roll around.

Bake the clafoutis until it is slightly puffed and lightly browned around the edges and the tomatoes are starting to burst, 45 to 50 minutes. Let cool for about 5 minutes (it will deflate a bit), then scoop out portions and eat while still warm; the clafoutis is also good at room temperature.

ROASTED CANNED TOMATOES

When my former colleague Matthew Card turned me on to the concept of roasting a *canned* tomato, my mind was blown. I had roasted every type of fresh tomato every way I knew, but I'd always thought a canned tomato could never be more than the slightly boring thing in a can—perfect in a sauce or stew, but nothing that you would roast and snack on!

But not so. You can scoop out the interior seeds and pulp and wipe off the canning juices from a canned tomato, leaving you with a mostly intact, hopefully very ripe plum tomato that will improve in flavor and texture after a few hours in the oven.

In the same way that a canned tomato is different from a ripe tomato fresh from the garden, roasted canned tomatoes will be different, and maybe not as luscious, as roasted fresh tomatoes. Your starting point is a tomato that was bred for canning, so uniformity won out over character and complexity, not to mention that a canned tomato has already been processed once. But despite all that, roasting a canned tomato takes it from slightly acidic and watery to sweet, concentrated, and almost chewy.

Managing the Variables

In this method, the main variable to manage is the canned tomato itself rather than the juices given off by fresh tomatoes during roasting. You're not likely to get a lot of juice from roasting canned tomatoes, and if you do, it won't be the sparkling bright nectar that can occur from fresh, so you can pretty much ignore the juices.

Your canned tomatoes must be mostly intact, so if you open the can and see that the tomatoes are sort of shredded or they fall apart in your fingers, find another use for them. Equally important, the tomatoes need to be ripe all the way through. Most decent brands will be both intact and ripe, but I have opened cans only to find sort of stringy pale orange tomatoes. Get to know a brand that you like and can trust, and they'll be fine for roasting.

Because canned tomatoes are so wet to start with, your mission is to eliminate as much of the liquid as possible before cooking, to give the tomatoes a chance to actually roast and not simply steam. You'll accomplish this by first sort of squeegeeing the liquid off them as you remove each tomato from the can and, second, by removing the seeds and pulp. The tomatoes will still be wet and slightly fragile, but have faith—they will firm up and even become chewy and dense, perfect for so many delicious destinations.

ROASTED CANNED TOMATOES

MAKES ABOUT 2 POUNDS (900 G)

Extra-virgin olive oil

Two 28-ounce (794 g) cans whole peeled tomatoes

Kosher salt

Preheat the oven to 300°F (150°C). Spread a thin layer of olive oil on a 13-by-18-inch (33 by 45 cm) sheet pan.

Lift a tomato from the can, gently pierce it to release the juice without spurting, and then coax out the seeds with your fingers. Give the tomato another little squeeze to extract more liquid but not so hard that you deform it. Arrange the tomato on the sheet pan and repeat with all the tomatoes, leaving a bit of room between them to allow air to circulate and dry them out. Save the juice for another use; it will freeze well for several months in a zip-top bag.

Drizzle the tomatoes generously with olive oil (but don't drown them, since you want them to dry out), and sprinkle lightly with salt.

Roast the tomatoes until they are much deeper in color, look drier, and feel almost chewy. They will still be quite moist and may start to caramelize around the edges, which is good, but don't let the browning become extreme, which would make them too bitter. Let the tomatoes cool a bit and then transfer to an airtight container, float a thin layer of olive oil on top, and store in the fridge for up to 2 weeks or in the freezer for up to 3 months.

Good Things to Do with Roasted Canned Tomatoes

Top some flatbread and sprinkle with za'atar seasoning; make a winter BLT with cooked escarole instead of lettuce; chop and add to a winter vegetable soup; chop and combine with chopped cooked shrimp and fold into paella-style rice (see page 205).

Tomato Pissaladière

This classic Provençale pastry is most often topped with just onion, olives, and anchovies, but to me, a tomato is the obvious fourth member of the band. Part pizza, part focaccia, a pissaladière wants enough topping to be delicious but not so much that the dough becomes overloaded and soggy. Make sure to let your tomatoes drain thoroughly before arranging them on the dough.

And about the dough. Here I'm using a yeasted dough that benefits from a 24-hour rise, but there are other options: store-bought bread dough or even puff pastry, which seems perhaps too fancy and out of character with this earthy southern French dish, yet the French very often make pissaladière with puff pastry. You could use Super-Flaky "Almost" Puff Pastry Dough (page 226) or store-bought frozen puff pastry.

Fun fact: while the name *pissaladière* sounds like it might relate to either pizza or salad or both, it actually comes from a type of anchovy paste made in the Mediterranean—*pissalat*—back in the day when the sea was chock-full of young anchovies.

MAKES ONE 13-BY-18 INCH (33 BY 45 CM) FLATBREAD

Dough

1 cup (130 g) all-purpose flour

½ cup (65 g) whole-grain flour, such as spelt or whole wheat

¾ cup (180 ml) warm water (100° to 110°F/38° to 43°C)

1 envelope (2¼ teaspoons/7 g) active dry yeast

3 tablespoons extra-virgin olive oil, plus more for the bowl

1 teaspoon kosher salt

Topping

Extra-virgin olive oil

1 very large or 2 smaller onions (about 12 ounces/340 g total), thinly sliced

4 or 5 garlic cloves, sliced

2 sprigs fresh rosemary

Kosher salt

continues

ABOUT 1 DAY AHEAD, MAKE THE DOUGH: In a stand mixer fitted with the dough hook or paddle attachment (or in a medium bowl, using a wooden spoon), combine the all-purpose and whole-grain flours.

In a small bowl, stir together the water, yeast, and olive oil. With the mixer running on low, pour the water mixture into the flour and let the mixer run on low for about 5 minutes (or stir by hand for a little longer).

Let the dough rest for about 10 minutes, then sprinkle in the salt and mix for another 5 minutes. Scoop out the dough and put it into a generously oiled bowl. Cover with plastic wrap and put it in the fridge for as close to 24 hours as is convenient for your schedule, but at least 12 hours.

UP TO 1 DAY AHEAD, COOK THE ONION FOR THE TOPPING: In a large skillet, heat a big glug of olive oil over medium heat. Add the onion, garlic, rosemary, and a big pinch of salt. Cook until the onion is soft and fragrant, 15 to 20 minutes; if the onion seems to be drying out during cooking, add a few spoonfuls of water, cover the pan, and steam until juicier. Once it's quite tender, turn up the heat a tiny bit and cook for another few minutes, stirring and scraping the pan, until it is a deeper golden and very sweet. Taste and add more salt, if you like (but remember that the

1 large or 2 medium tomatoes (about 12 ounces/340 g total), cored

One 2-ounce (60 g) can anchovy fillets, drained

10 to 15 pitted Kalamata olives, halved

½ cup (50 g) finely grated Parmigiano-Reggiano cheese

anchovies will be salty). Discard the rosemary sprigs (it's okay if some leaves remain in the onion) and set aside to cool.

About 1 hour before you want to bake the pissaladière, take the dough from the refrigerator and let it come to room temperature. It should be puffy and doubled in size at this point.

Preheat the oven to 450°F (230°C).

Very thinly slice the tomatoes. Arrange on a cooling rack set over a sheet pan to catch the juices, salt lightly, and leave to drain. (If you don't have a cooling rack, just spread the slices on the sheet pan.)

Lightly oil a 13-by-18 inch (33 by 45 cm) sheet pan. Scrape the dough from the bowl onto the sheet pan and gently press it out to form an even layer; the dough is slightly wet and sticky and may be a bit elastic and not want to stay where you put it. If so, just let it rest for a few more minutes. As it warms up, it should relax. Try to get all the way into the corners of the pan, but it's okay if the dough shrinks back a bit.

When the dough is stretched out properly, distribute the onion over the surface. Blot the tomato slices on paper towels to dry off surface juice and arrange them on the onion.

Arrange the anchovies (taste them first, and if they're super salty, give them a quick rinse and a blot dry) on the tomatoes and then scatter the olives over everything. Drizzle with more olive oil and bake for about 15 minutes.

Shower the pissaladière with the grated Parmigiano and continue baking until the dough is light golden brown on the edges and underside, the tomatoes are slightly sizzling and browned, and everything looks very Mediterranean, another 5 to 10 minutes.

Gently slide the pissaladière from the sheet pan onto a cooling rack and, if you like (which I generally do), drizzle on a bit more good olive oil and let cool for a few minutes. Cut into squares and serve right away. Keep any leftovers for a day, well-wrapped, in the fridge, and reheat them loosely wrapped in foil in a 375°F (190°C) oven until hot.

Or Try This Idea

Increase the focus on the toppings: instead of fresh tomato, top the pissaladière with Roasted Canned Tomatoes (page 235), using an amount that gives you plenty but doesn't swamp the dough. You'll want to split any large tomatoes into smaller pieces. As soon as you remove the baked pissaladière from the oven, drizzle on about ½ cup (120 ml) pesto.

Resources

For reliable information on how to can the tomatoes, sauces, jams, and pickles in this book:

BallMasonJars.com

I get inspiration and tips from these folks on their various websites and social media:

GrowBetterVeggies.com, the website for Love Apple Farms, a gardening and cooking educational center near Santa Cruz, California, run by attorney turned farmer Cynthia Sandberg.

Tomatomania.com, run by Scott Daigre, a tomato fanatic and garden designer who runs a test garden in Ojai, California; his Instagram account, **@tomatomania**, is a thrill.

WorldTomatoSociety.com, the website for a community of passionate tomato growers, both pros and home gardeners, with a searchable database, informative articles, and opportunities to connect with other tomato lovers.

This is the cannery that produces the excellent canned tomatoes referenced on page 29:

Stanislaus.com. The website and their Instagram account post super-fun videos.

To learn more about genuine San Marzanos, along with a few other Italian delectables:

ConsorzioPM.com/en

To explore the fascinating world of umami:

Visit the excellent website produced by a Japanese nonprofit that was established to promote the scientific understanding of "the fifth taste": **UmumiInfo.com**

To read more from food science writer Harold McGee on eating tomato leaves:

Read his **Curious Cook** column in the *New York Times* from July 28, 2009.

Acknowledgments

I HAVE SO MUCH AFFECTION AND GRATITUDE FOR THE TEAM AT ARTISAN—Lia Ronnen, Judy Pray (my brilliant editor), Allison McGeehon, Zach Greenwald, Sibylle Kazeroid, Suet Chong, Jane Treuhaft, Nancy Murray, Donna G. Brown, and Brooke Beckmann. Thanks to Toni Tajima for the super book design, and to my funny and smart and supportive agent, Joy Tutela.

WARM THANKS TO Helen Baldus and Kate Lebo for their excellent recipe testing. I hope the three of us can cook together in person some day; we will cause a tasty ruckus.

AND OF COURSE ENDLESS THANKS TO MY WONDERFUL PHOTOGRAPHY TEAM: Ellen Silverman, my best friend for thirty years, who makes the most gorgeous images and runs a photo shoot with grace and humor, and Nora Singley (with Alyssa Kondracki), whose talent makes my food look so casually delectable.

Index

MARTHA HOLMBERG is a food writer who has authored or co-authored nine cookbooks. *Modern Sauces* was a James Beard Award finalist. *Six Seasons: A New Way with Vegetables*, written with chef Joshua McFadden, won the James Beard Award, and *Grains for Every Season*, also with McFadden, was a James Beard Award finalist.

Holmberg was the editor in chief of *Fine Cooking* magazine for a decade, the food editor of *The Oregonian* newspaper in Portland, Oregon, and the founder of *MIX* magazine. She studied cooking at La Varenne in Paris, where she worked for several years as a private chef. She lives with her partner, John, in beautiful Spokane, Washington, where they grow too many tomatoes and otherwise spend as much time as possible on Nordic skis or with fly rods in their hands. Follow her on Instagram at @marthaholmberg.